NT POWER

DATE DUE

POSITIVE
PARENT POWER

A 7-part programme

Helen Bethune

THORSONS PUBLISHING GROUP

First published 1991

Copyright © Helen Bethune 1991

British Library Cataloguing in Publication Data

Bethune, Helen
Positive parent power: a 7-part
programme.
1. Parenthood
I. Title
306.874

ISBN 0 7225 2137 5

Published by Thorsons Publishers Limited, Wellingborough, Northamptonshire NN8 2RQ, England

Typeset by Harper Phototypesetters Limited, Northampton, England
Printed in Great Britain by Hartnolls Limited, Bodmin, Cornwall

1 3 5 7 9 10 8 6 4 2

Contents

Acknowledgements

MY SPECIAL THANKS . . . to Anna Williams for having faith in the work, even when I flagged.

And to Robert Dudley and Deborah Gemmell — two wise and constructive editors.

I want to thank the many (anonymous) parents who have wittingly, and sometimes unwittingly contributed.

And last, my sons — Alex and Andy and Angus, who really were the first cause!

Introduction

In the parents' best interests

You can't take a university course to learn how to be a good parent. We are supposed to know intuitively how to do it. By an unfortunate oversight, full instructions do not come with the product. Babies arrive with apparently only three built-in requirements: 'Feed me, love me, protect me'. Beyond that, parents are on their own.

In every library and bookshop there's a mass of information if you want to find out what to do for your children. You can read up about nappy rash or the terrible two's, about preparing them for school or coping with the teens. Any problem in your child, there's advice by the yard.

But who cares for parents? Being a parent is a high-profile occupation. Parents are constantly told how important they are and what a valuable job they do, raising the next generation. Yet in all sorts of ways, parents are discounted and put down in our society. When there is any trouble concerning young people, fingers always point at parents: 'If only parents would . . .' 'Parents could do more . . .' 'Parents should do more . . .'. Whatever the circumstances, parents ar supposed to know what to do for the best. They 'should' get it right. That's their job.

Unfortunately an increasing number of parents don't feel they know how to get it right, often do *not* know what to do for the best. All good parents want the same in the end for their children. They want them to be happy and fulfilled. But there's a creeping failure of nerve, an increasing loss of assurance. The old imperial base 'I'm your parent and what I say goes' has been ripped away. No

9

great loss, perhaps – but what do we put in its place? In council houses and in stately homes children are often difficult to control and many parents are unsure of themselves. In a crucial sense, they feel unsupported.

For several decades, the accepted way of looking at the parent-child relationship has been to concentrate on the child. Attention is focused on what seems to be 'the child's best interests'. In this book, you and I are doing something different. We are going to take the spotlight off children, and give our full attention to the other half of the equation: parents. We are concerned here with *the parents' best interests*.

Mixed messages

Becoming a parent means making a social contract. When you increase the population, society automatically gets a stake in your life in ways that did not happen when you were child-free. In return for accepting the new member, society dumps a whole bag of duties on the hapless parents. The biggest is the job of preparing the child for its place in the wider society. Fair enough. But these days society keeps changing the rules. The world our parents and grandparents prepared for us was a very different place to the world our children have inherited. Parents these days sometimes can't even find the goal-posts.

Once upon a time children were brought up according to the established customs and morality of the society their parents happened to live in. Values and traditions were accepted and agreed by everyone. If you stepped out of line, you knew what to expect. Society told you loud and clear. In traditional societies this still obtains today.

But in the last 30 years many cherished values have bitten the dust. Public attitudes to the family, the church, the police, the courts, to education, to sex, and to work – all have changed or fragmented. Our society now speaks with forked tongue, and it makes being a parent a very difficult task.

Let's take an example: sex before marriage. In our grand-parent's time this was forbidden for girls, manly for boys. Daughters who flouted the rule (and were found out) were disgraced. Most parents followed through with severe sanctions, or themselves suffered social stigma. Quite often the girl was flung on the streets.

Nowadays there is no general agreement. Parents have to decide for themselves what rules they would like their children to follow. They can opt for contraception and abortion, or for virginity until the bridal night – or anything in between. They sometimes just ignore the whole thing and hope for the best. Society gives no firm rules, endorses no specific attitude, and the kids know it. For responsible parents, this is a heavy burden. It does not stop with sex. Individual parents have to think through, and act on, all manner of issues.

Today's dread issues

Issues, furthermore, which must have our grandparents spinning in their graves. They had their problems of course – but they certainly didn't have to cope with heroin, crack and glue-sniffing behind the bike sheds, as well as cheap booze in every corner-shop and supermarket. Parents today cannot ignore the new dreadful spectre of AIDS. Nor can they overlook the growing evidence of child abuse. Nobody knows how prevalent this was in the past. Nobody knows how prevalent it is today. But few thinking people would deny the possibility that pornographic videos have turned some fantasizers into activists. There were no porno or snuff videos available for our parents' and grandparents' living rooms.

Parents who are not affluent have new problems. The school leaving age has gone remorselessly up this century, and the effects of this can severely undermine family goodwill as well as family budgets.

Increasing numbers of young people dossing in the streets of our great cities also bears witness to much grave family distress. That this has been accepted at a public level can be deduced from the chilling fact that in 1988 some central London Underground stations displayed posters with the message, 'Left home? Let your family know how you are. No need to say *where* you are'.

With all this, it's hardly surprising that parents often feel inadequate. We have not been prepared to deal with these new questions. We stagger on from problem to problem, cobbling together solutions for ourselves and hoping against hope that we've made the right decision. Quite often we doubt it. If something – anything – goes wrong, many parents assume they are to blame for making the 'wrong' decision.

Most parents lack a sense of being supported, of being valued.

Seldom does a week go by without some expert busybody proclaiming that the nation is imperilled in one way or another because parents aren't doing their job properly. But at the same time, more years are tacked onto 'childhood' – and every home with television is bombarded with merchandise which we could or should buy for our children to give them added advantages over everyone else's children.

A confusion of experts

Instead of support there are experts. Experts always know better than parents. Unfortunately, due to their numbers and variety, they have confused things even more. Every decade or two, some of these experts go out of fashion and new ones emerge to take their place. Let me tell you what happened about my eldest son's reading. Reading is, after all, something we all have to learn, and today parents are encouraged to have children reading (if possible) even before they start school.

Two decades ago it was different. I went to register my firstborn, then aged 4, at the local school. At the little boy's request – (and doing as my own mother had done), I had started to teach him to read. The Head was aghast. He insisted I stop. My methods were quite out of date, he said. I would only confuse the child. He added ominously that if I did succeed, Alex would be ahead of the other children and would get bored. What could be worse than that? In fact what befell was a lot worse. By a quirk of staff changes, Alex experienced three teachers in five terms and each of the teachers used a different 'new' teaching method. There was Look and Say, the phonic method – and another the name of which now escapes me. You will not be suprised to learn that Alex didn't read fluently till he was nearly seven. He suffered – but so did I. I was left with a real but confused sense of guilt that somehow I'd let my child down, that I hadn't acted rightly by him.

Every parent has a story of confusion by experts. Anita provided a classic example. She told the tale with wry amusement. On the third day her newly born infant wailed non-stop. Anita asked the midwife what could be the matter? 'You must be underfeeding her' was the response. When the night staff came on, the infant was still raising the roof. Anita asked the question again. 'You must be overfeeding her' replied the night nurse.

Experts often seem to have axes to grind. Sometimes their work is exploited for purposes which do not help individual parents.

The research of John Bowlby just after World War Two, was concerned with grossly deprived babies. It was widely interpreted as showing that less than full-time mothering would result in seriously disturbed children. This research was certainly used to steer women out of the workplace so jobs could be given to men demobbed from the Forces. A great many perfectly good mothers who had to work to support their families were given a huge extra burden of guilt, much of which still lingers on today. Yet throughout human history, in all societies, women have done the lion's share of providing food for the family (the primary work of keeping the race alive) while older children, relatives, or 'aunties' have taken over the child-minding. The upper classes for at least three centuries have cheerfully handed over their young to domestic help and institutions without any noticeable burden of guilt.

Conscientious parents have many, many more decisions to make today in bringing up their young than ever before in history. Look at some other matters which have been kicked around by experts in the last thirty years or so: the presence of fathers during the birth, home or hospital births, feeding on demand, potty training, working mothers, help with homework, homework at all, Saturday jobs, competitive sport, examinations, school uniforms, sex education, religious instruction. And this is only the surface stuff. Major social changes have seriously undermined the whole enterprise of parenting – but the bottom line is that parents are still left holding the baby.

A job update

Today we do not grind our own corn and send messages by beacon from hill to hill, but the work of parenting is still swathed in romantic myths which have little to do with life in the last decades of the twentieth century. *We need an update on the job description*. The world has changed – and it's time we reconsidered what can properly be expected of parents today.

What are realistic goals? What are our duties, our rights, our responsibilities? What are – (dreadful word) – our parameters? Have we adequate resources for the job?

In thinking through these questions, it became clear to me that parents – ordinary parents – have far more resources than most of us ever realized. Since time began, parents have had no less than seven huge, primeval powers and these powers are still available to us today. Properly applied, these powers enable us, not to become superparents (who needs that?) – but to be comfortable and easy about the job we have to do, as indeed nature intended. That's what this book is about: rediscovering for ourselves how to use our basic resources as parents.

So this book is for and about parents. We've all heard – and probably used – the glum refrain 'Parents can't win' – but actually it turns out somewhat differently. Parents *can* win. Parents can reclaim their nerve and their confidence in doing a good job well. We have the means, as you will see as you read on. I'm not suggesting it is easy – but then it isn't easy when we *don't* get it right. It may involve looking at things from a slightly different angle, and very probably doing some re-thinking about our attitudes and behaviour.

The great thing is that it's never too late. No matter what the age or stage of your child or yourself, change is possible. In point of fact, change is inevitable. Like it or not, we are all changing all the time. What we do not always remember is that we have power to decide *how* we change. We are not hostages to our personal history. We can stop the rot here and now – if we choose.

Archaic, given powers

Being a parent is a state of mind, a social condition, and a whole uncharted universe of emotions. It is intensely personal and intimate, yet at the same time it is publicly defining. In some ways it is very like marriage. But there is a difference – for parenthood reaches far, far back into the dawn of time, long before there was any 'marrying' or 'giving in marriage'. And when we come to look, we find that nature herself has supplied us with all the necessary resources to make a decent job of it. It may surprise you to learn that you use all of them anyway in your everyday life – just by being a parent. Here, then is the list:

1. Biological Power
2. Legitimate Power
3. Dynastic Power
4. Coercive Power
5. Reward Power
6. Moral Power
7. Personal Power

Quite impressive, yes? Spelled out like this, we can see why people think that merely having a child endows us with the wisdom to cope. It doesn't, of course. It merely gives us power.

And here is the first catch. Power of itself is neutral. Any power can be used creatively or destructively. To be an effective parent, we need to know how to use specific powers in the right time and in the right way. If we get it wrong, power can turn very nasty on us.

Taking each in turn, we will see how, appropriately used, these powers really work in the day-to-day business of being a parent – whatever the stage or age of your child or children. We will also observe how their misuse causes many familiar parental problems. We will also find out that the great social changes in this century have altered their relative importance. Some have been diminished, others expanded. But when we come to examine them, it is clear that every aspect of being a good parent flows naturally from them – our goals, duties, rights, responsibilities, rewards – even the fringe benefits.

As we now start to examine our basic resources as parents, we shall also set them in historical context so that we can see clearly what is really appropriate today. As we go along, we shall take note of new skills developed by a variety of parents. We will consider strategies and tactics – some as old as time, some with more recent origins in psychology, sociology, and management studies. What has been found to work effectively in other parts of our lives may be usefully applied to our job as parents – certainly the sharp end of social relations. We are aiming for guidelines, not cut-and-dried answers. Every parent is unique, every family is different, and we can each work only within our personal framework.

Massive changes have been taking place in our society and in our lives. That is why so many parents and children are showing signs of stress. We need to think about what we are doing in the light of our own history and today's world. We owe this to our children as well as to ourselves. When we understand our resources properly we can get a sound perspective on the job. It's also a matter of enlightened self-interest. Here is no guarantee of instant 'Happy Families' – but there is a promise of increased self-assurance on the job. And that is no small thing.

BIOLOGICAL POWER

*'Good parenting quite often means learning to recognize
and override our innate primitive instincts'*

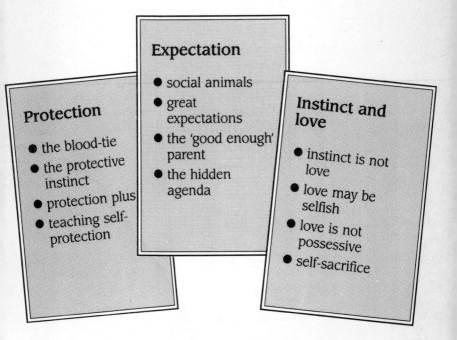

Expectation

- social animals
- great expectations
- the 'good enough' parent
- the hidden agenda

Protection

- the blood-tie
- the protective instinct
- protection plus
- teaching self-protection

Instinct and love

- instinct is not love
- love may be selfish
- love is not possessive
- self-sacrifice

Protection

Our first resource is the biological power – that force which enables parents to move mountains, to go to any lengths, to sacrifice life itself for their child. The key concern of the biological power is protection of the species. It is strongest when our child is weakest.

The blood-tie

It is the primary physical bond, the blood-tie, which draws its awesome strength from our very species' determination to survive. It drives us into wanting to produce children, and uses the magic of sex to make sure we follow through and preserve our kind.

The myths of Oedipus, Cain and Medea strike dark and terrible resonances in us because they involve destruction of mother, brother, children. Human beings seldom destroy those who share the same bloodlines. Although most murders are domestic, recent analyses of statistics in the UK have shown that hardly any occur between actual blood relatives. Murders involve husbands, wives, step-relations, lovers, enemies, rivals, in-laws – but rarely those who are linked by blood.

Some research suggests that the individual blood-tie may be genetically inbuilt. A team of scientists working at the University of Washington in 1978 reported the results of experiments with 16 young rhesus monkeys: They appeared to have an inborn ability to recognize close relatives they had never encountered before in their lives. The test involved half-brothers and half-sisters, each of whom was related only on the father's side (thus ruling out the possibility of them having picked up some special family smell in the womb). The monkeys were taken at birth from their families, and reared with other monkeys. Then all the 16 test monkeys, of differing ages, were simultaneously introduced to a collection of monkeys, some of whom were their own half-sisters or half-brothers on their father's side. To the astonishment of the scientists, 13 of the 16 monkeys chose freely to join their blood relatives rather than other, unrelated monkeys. Age and sex made no difference. The scientists are still trying to figure out the implications of this astonishing evidence from the animal world which appears to bear out the old saying that 'blood is thicker than water'.

The mysterious permanent link

The blood-tie is a force which works two ways. Its original thrust is for the preservation of the species – hence when a child is newborn, engaging, and defenceless, it propels *parents* into essential caretaking. As the child grows, develops, and becomes adult, human parents – like parents in other species – cease to be driven by the biological tie. Gradually they release their young from the close parental protection which helpless infancy required. As far as nature is concerned, the job is done. The future of the race is supposedly assured.

But for human *children* things are a bit different. From the beginning a child is tied to its parents or caretaker. Every child is physically dependent on its parents (or caretaker parents) for protection for several years after birth. But emotionally, we seem to be forever linked, mysteriously but indissolubly, to our parents by blood. Present or absent, alive or dead, known or unknown, loved or rejected, our parents inhabit our lives and our dreams. Thus, in the psyche and the personality of our children, parents willy-nilly achieve a kind of immortality. This gives them a sizeable, if often unrecognized power-base.

The protective instinct

It is clear that the primary duty of parents is to provide protection for our children. This is an imperative of our species and accounts for the superhuman strength given to the father whose child was trapped under an overturned car. Without help he lifted the car and freed his child. It accounts also for the unexpected courage which enabled a timid mother of two sleeping infants to confront – and rout – two burglars in her home. Less spectacularly, it gives us eyes in the back of our head when a toddler is about to cross a busy street. It gives us the wit to look ahead and foresee possible perils – a sharp knife, a box of matches, broken glass, medicines in reach of small, exploring hands. These dangers are today's sabre-toothed tigers. Built into the protective duty are many essential resources to enable us to carry it out.

Longer childhood

But because our society has changed so radically, it is not only our enemies which are different today. Childhood itself is different now – in that it is about half as long again. Hitherto, in all so-cieties children came of age at around twelve or thirteen. Most traditional societies have transition rites at puberty when boys are inducted into the world of men, girls into the secrets of women. The BarMitzvah ritual of the Jews is a classic example.

But with the invention of schooling and (more or less) universal education up till the age of eighteen or beyond, the years of dependence are greatly prolonged. This complicates parenting as we actually have to supply the appropriate care. Let us go back again to the original purpose of our biological power. Its primary purpose is to provide the young child with what the child cannot physically provide for itself to survive in the world. In its pure form it is not love but instinct, very like sexual infatuation. It is, how-ever, a power of diminishing returns. As the child grows it needs less and less protection in different areas. Toddlers cannot cross streets alone. Older children can. Your 11 year old can probably travel on public transport without adult protection in the daytime – although it is doubtful if a good parent would allow him or her out on the streets alone after dark. This power almost inevitably gets used less and less as the child grows. When it is used at an inappropriate stage of a child's development, more often than not it turns out to be actively damaging.

Overprotection can destroy

If you find yourself saying (or even thinking), 'He's my flesh and blood, I'll stick by him whatever he does', you can be sure biological power is dictating the shots, and it may be time to look at what you are doing – and your real motivation. Take the case of Donald and Fiona, and their student son, James. These parents continued to protect their son long past the time when he was perfectly capable of looking after himself. The results, as you will see, were almost catastrophic.

On the surface they appeared to be a fortunate family – until you learnt what went on behind the front door of their comfortable home. Donald was a director in a thriving firm of accountants. Fiona worked in public relations. When James was 20, they discovered he was dependent on drugs.

For at least a year before this disclosure, both Fiona and Donald had allowed themselves to be manipulated into giving and 'lending' money to James, money which of course they never got back. Both independently wrote off thefts and losses and told lies to each other – to cover up for James. Both accepted countless promises that were always broken, countless excuses that didn't add up. Their nights were fragmented by telephone calls from strange people at strange hours, and in endless agonizing over what and why and how everything had gone so wrong.

James came and went unpredictably, assuring them he was getting to lectures, doing his essays. He was moody – sometimes aggressive and threatening, sometimes fragile and nervous, sometimes withdrawn. For long periods he would remain alone in his horrible, messy room. He would allow no one in. Because they so desperately wanted it to be true, they accepted his assurances that he was working.

All this took a terrible toll on Donald and Fiona, who could not understand how their beloved son had changed into this tormented monster. Their own relationship began to fall apart, and James – in the grip of his compulsion – worked on the rift: separate, the parents would cough up more. To his mother he would explain that his 'problems' really began at school. (His father had insisted on that school.) To his father he would say his problems really came from his relationship with his mother – it was so difficult being an only child. (Fiona hadn't been able to have any more children.)

When his first court case was coming up, James promised to reform, and once more, his parents accepted his promise and stood by him, bending the truth more than a little in James' defence. 'You can't just let your own flesh and blood go to prison if there's any way you can help', Fiona said defiantly.

Through his parents' 'protection' James got off.

And of course, James went on using. The troubles increased. There was another court case – this time a fine, and on at least two occasions his parents paid off hefty debts to dealers. Driven by misdirected biological power, Donald and Fiona feather-bedded their son's heroin habit. Time and again James promised to mend his ways. But he couldn't stay 'off' – because his parents made his 'using' so comfortable. Effectively Donald and Fiona were subsidizing his drugs, though they believed they were protecting him from even greater dangers such as prison, a beating up or even suicide – which more than once he threatened. He persuaded them that he would be fine if he went back to college, with a flat of his own and some security. Within a month there was a call from the local police. James was in hospital. He was in intensive care following an overdose.

In despair the parents sought advice in a self-help group of other families who had suffered as they were suffering. They had, they felt, done everything humanly possible for their son. Where had they gone wrong? They felt they had failed but they also felt betrayed. They were terrified James would die – yet there were moments when they almost wished he would. They felt fearful, desolate, angry, guilty, frustrated, shamed.

The suggestions they were given upturned all their ingrained beliefs and habits. First to go was guilt. They were helped to understand that they were *not* responsible for James' abuse of drugs. His decision to use was his own. At 13, when he tried his first joint, he knew perfectly well it was both illegal and danger-ous. In no way had his parents incited or encouraged his drug-taking – whatever James might say. Only James could stop it, because only James had started it.

It was pointed out that in their zeal to be 'good' parents, they had put up with behaviour from their son which they would not have tolerated from anyone else. By protecting him from the consequences of his own decisions, they had effectively infantil-ized the young man. While Fiona and Donald did the worrying for him, why should James worry? They were advised to start minding their *own* business, to put their *own* lives in order – and to get out of 'the protection racket'.

Painfully they began to assess their own behaviour. They wanted James to learn to say 'no' to drugs – but what example had they given him? Whenever he begged and pleaded, they'd turned their own no's into grudging but definite 'yes's. Like James, they would have to start learning to say 'no' and stick to it. They wanted James to be honest – had they always been honest? The parents admitted they had lied to each other, to the police, to the court, to friends, to neighbours, to the family.

Even more painfully they each looked at the motives for their actions. Wasn't there a lot of shame and hurt pride lurking around? What (for example) would the family say? What would the neighbours say? Of course there's nothing wrong with discretion and family pride – in the right place and time. But at this time and place secrecy was actually endangering James' life. As long as James believed he was getting away with it, he didn't have to do anything about the habit that would certainly put his life at risk.

In accepting James' lies and promises, both parents had hoped to manipulate him into leading the life *they* wanted for him. But their efforts had achieved nothing. James was worse than ever. They were powerless to control him. They could only live their own lives, not his.

In the following months, Fiona and Donald waged war against their old habits. They told James he could no longer live rent-free. Two weeks later, when no rent was forthcoming, they said he'd have to find somewhere else to live. They made it clear they knew he was still using – and said that if he could find the money for drugs, he could certainly find money for rent. They also made it clear that they would help him when he really wanted to come off. Donald gave him a list of addresses of helping agencies. James tore it up and departed in a furious temper.

He moved in with addict friends, and went from bad to worse. When he visited his parents (either to scrounge or to abuse them) he was wrecked and wasted. But finally he reached the end of his tether. He'd run out of friends and he had to face the awful truth that even his parents – the last resort – were no longer willing to put up with him. He was forced to take responsibility for his own life. He asked for the list.

So James began the long haul back to sanity and life. But Donald and Fiona's recovery had already begun. They found themselves experiencing a new peace and freedom once they stopped trying to be responsible for their son's life – once they stopped inappropriately protecting their adult son. While they had allowed themselves to be driven by blind instinct they were unsuccessful as parents and uncomfortable as people. When they got round to being honest, both admitted that the theory, 'My child right or wrong' had led them to act in ways that were not very honourable and from motives which were less than worthy.

I have given this story at length because it is a stark illustration of the consequences of the inappropriate use of a parental power. But biological power is a very strong and primitive instinct which is part of the kit issued to all parents. It turns up all over the place. We all recognize the mother who insists on collecting her 12 year old son from school by car when all his friends are using the bus. We've met the father who puts his daughter's casual tennis partner through a third degree, and the parent who assumes, automatically, that a bad school report is a product of teacher prejudice – not of their child's laziness. All of these are examples of overprotectiveness – and nobody is really taken in. The son knows his mother craves his company – not his welfare; the daughter knows daddy isn't interested in the suitability of her tennis partner – *no* partner would satisfy this father; the lazy child knows he is lazy and isn't specially proud of himself for conning his mother – he also is quite aware of her weakness, she cannot bear failure in *her* child.

At root the protective aspect of biological power acts like an extension of the instinct of self-preservation. At birth, a new baby *is* very like an extension of the mother's body – but many parents act as if their children were continuing extensions of themselves. Good parenting quite often means learning to recognize and override our innate primitive instincts.

Protection plus

Protection alone is not enough. It is also our job to teach our children self-protection, just as animals do for their young.

Now that the taboos on incest and sexual abuse of children have been publicly breached, it is plain they have not been working at all in some families. Many children, of both sexes, have been gravely, permanently, damaged. How widespread this is, and has been, is impossible to know. There is no firm evidence. Society is at present reacting with shocked horror – but for a recognizable time in our society, childhood has been professionally sexualized.

The most pervasive influence on modern psychological thought has been Sigmund Freud. His observations and theories have infiltrated not only the psychiatric and 'caring' professions, but even the consciousness and mythology of ordinary everyday people. Who has not heard of the Oedipus complex? Of Freudian slips? It is known that Freud was appalled when he first realized the prevalence and persistence of incestuous attacks by their fathers on his female patients in respectable, bourgeois Vienna. For reasons which have never been satisfactorily explained, Freud decided to conceal the findings. In fact he even made a *volte face* and propounded the bizarre theory that infant girls harbour libidinous fantasies about their fathers. And all little boys, he stated, have sexual designs on their mothers – following the mythic example of Oedipus who inadvertently killed his father and unknowingly married his mother. From this farrago of fantasies (from a man known to have had a cocaine habit) has grown a whole industry dedicated to the proposition that babies and children are primarily sexual creatures almost all of whose behaviour is sexually motivated.

The plain fact is that the arrival of the menses in girls, and the dropping of testicles in boys are physical statements that a child is ready for adult sexual activity. Before that time, children's interest in genitalia is no more or less significant than their interest in ears, teeth or toes. Exploration – by way of 'nurses or doctors' or 'mummies and daddies' – or the 'I'll show you if you show me' variety is just that: exploration. Children are immensely curious. They've a lot of learning to do. They can hardly fail to realize that adults place great emphasis (positive or negative) on sexual matters. Interested? Of course they're interested.

Until puberty, so-called coquettish or flirtatious behaviour is entirely in the eye of the beholder. All children mimic their elders. It is how they learn. A small girl who observes her mother using her eyelashes or legs to win a cuddle from daddy will try out similar behaviour towards available and beloved males. The mistake is to put an adult-centred interpretation upon it. A child without experience cannot possibly envisage consequences beyond a loving hug.

This book is not addressed to parents who have gross personal problems such as involve the sexual abuse of children, or complicity in the act. Nonetheless, the possibility of this happening to any of our children is something parents have always had to consider.

From personal experience and observation, it seems to me there are several simple but important things which we can do to help our children preserve the inviolability of their bodies.

Teaching children self-protection

1. We can listen to them. When a child particularly does not want to have dealings with any adult, we need to respect that wish – however inconvenient it may be. It is hard enough for an adult to explain an intuition: for a child it may be well-nigh impossible. But children's intuitions are usually trustworthy. Take no chances. Believe your child, even if he or she can't say why.

2. We can discourage flirtatiousness in our pre-pubertal daughters and sons. It is possible to suggest firmly that showing off is not particularly attractive. This may be deflating, and perhaps not good for the ego of a future thespian, but it is far, far better to be safe than sorry. Don't dress little children as jail-bait. The world out there is not safe today. There is a strong case to be made for clothes and shoes they can run in. There's a lot to be said for karate classes.

3. Teaching children to protect themselves means helping them to develop personal boundaries, personal taboos. By our actions, we must show them that their bodies are their own. In the way we act with them we teach them the sanctity of their own bodies. Even our kisses matter. If you are accustomed to kiss your child on the mouth (as some parents do) – think again. In our society, kissing on the mouth is a conventional prelude to sexual activity. A child who is used to being kissed on the lips by mummy and daddy, may not recognize danger signals when he or she is kissed on the lips by that charming, closet pederast, Uncle Harold. A child whose mouth remains its own is a safer child.

In terms of general safety, all youngsters need to know that flight may be wiser than fight. But recognizing danger signals and having the confidence to trust their own instincts are the first essentials. Helping them to do this is an imperative which flows from our biological power.

Expectation

Social animals

Unlike other animals humans need to be socialized. The rest of the animal kingdom operates almost wholly on instinct. But humans act and behave, talk, and even think according to their social group. If you took a newborn Eskimo baby and brought it up in a Polynesian family in the South Seas, it would grow up with the world-view of a Polynesian. It would walk, talk, speak, and act in Polynesian fashion. Most anthropologists and ethologists agree that this is the factor which makes us distinctively human. Recent discoveries that chimps also socialize their young in ways previously considered specifically human has presented the scientific community with something of a dilemma, but a solution has been put forward which may still accommodate the theory – and take account of the chimps as well. It is suggested that chimps be upgraded – reclassified as hominids – not quite homo sapiens, but near enough to allow the theory to remain intact.

The society we live in determines our behaviour, our manners, our morals, our ways of thinking, our gods, our food, our dress, our customs, our attitudes. It even shapes in a general way the size of our families. Our biological power is very definitely modified by society. To see how quickly and easily people adapt the size of their families to local custom, we need only examine the fertility rates of migrants to countries like Britain from cultures where large families are the norm. By the second generation, average family size had dropped to the average level of the host country. The reasons (economic security, less need for hands to work the land, etc.) are not relevant here. The point is that a biological instinct has been modified by social conditions. More crudely, the Chinese and Indian governments have been trying for some years with limited success to depress birthrates – the Chinese by a mixture of stick and carrot to encourage one child families, the Indians by heavily promoting sterilization and vasectomy.

Our society today is very different from the one we inherited at the beginning of this century. We do not need to have large families, because we no longer have high infant mortality. Most of our children will survive, because we have – (most of us) – clean water, good drains, adequate food, shelter, maternity care, and medical protection against most of the child-killing diseases.

We also have more accessible and effective contraception, although in every society there have been contraceptive medicines and abortifacients – whether publicly acknowledged or not. When they failed, some societies have resorted to infanticide. Exposure as an unwanted newborn baby was the lot of Oedipus – but his fate has befallen many other very real children in many parts of the world, particularly where society values male children above female. Female infanticide is not unknown today.

But underneath all the social pulls and tugs, there remains the biological drive for humans to have children and to cherish and protect them. It is as inevitable for most humans to want children as it is to want food, water, shelter, and a mate. What is more, even when society makes it difficult and confusing for us to rear them, we have in ourselves sufficient powers to cope.

It is inevitable that we reflect our social conditioning in the way we act as parents. It simply is not possible for us to pursue a totally independent course. We act or react in direct response both to our own upbringing and to the pressures of society around us. We'll see this even more clearly as we go along.

Great expectations

The second aspect of biological power is that of expectations. This starts operating the moment a baby is on the way. We do after all *expect* a baby. Most babies are the products of mixed motives – an expression of love between a married couple being only the most socially acceptable reason. A 21 year old mother, Jane, was quoted recently in a Sunday newspaper. 'A lot of young girls are having babies now – it's something good they can have. Some-

29

thing they can love.' Babies are conceived to fill a gap, to provide a sibling, to repair a marriage, to hook a man, to keep a woman, to enable a girl to escape her first family – sometimes to get housing. A baby may be the result of love, fear, drugs, drink, poverty, ignorance, or rape.

It is therefore very wily of nature to make babies so beguiling. The old adage, 'Every baby brings its own love' usually turns out to be true. And like it or not, every baby also brings its own expectations.

The 'good enough parent'

The first expectation is of ourselves. For reasons which remain obscure, many new parents, particularly those in stable relationships, expect that they will naturally and inevitably turn out to be excellent parents. *They* will not make the perceived mistakes of their own parents, friends, and relatives. The futility of some of these expectations usually dawns quite quickly – often after a couple of sleepness nights. Fatigue is a great leveller.

On the other hand, most parents continue to expect far too much of themselves. Awed by the stupendous responsibility of this new, complete, and (sometimes) very demanding small person, we try to get everything just right. It should be noted that babies do not come into the world entirely defenceless. They have lungs. When a baby wants something it opens its mouth and roars. This sound acts rather like a dog whistle – sometimes barely audible to others, but inescapable for parents. Many a mother actually experiences a sharp, fierce pang in the womb or breasts when her young infant expresses its displeasure. For these reasons, parents are galvanized to try to perform miracles of planning and provision. Too often when they don't come off, we are disproportionately desolate at our seeming 'failures'. Many of us continue to expect the impossible of ourselves for years. A great many parents haven't yet got wind of the Winnicot's comforting theory of 'the good enough mother'. This eminent child psychologist, and his distinguished successor, Bruno Bettelheim, have at last gained for parents official permission to be fallible. It is now acknowledged that children can thrive and develop even if their parents are less than perfect. Having been systematically put down by analysts and psychologists since Freud first put pen to paper, parents need no longer agonize over every mistake or misjudgement, every sin of omission or commission. Kids are great survivors – and they know when they are loved.

Very often our feelings of failure come from a distorted sense of responsibility. We expect to control results, and many parents actually feel they are to blame when things don't turn out as planned. When we realize that we can only make the best decision open to us – and accept that we cannot be in charge of the final outcome, we can stop giving ourselves a hard time over it.

Alan and Heather's son Simon was a very well-adjusted little boy of 10, good at schoolwork and games and very popular at his local primary school. Some of his friends were going on to a large comprehensive, while others were enrolled at a small church comprehensive in the area. Having looked at both schools, talked to both Head Teachers, and discussed it with Simon, the parents decided that the boy would have better academic and sports opportunities at the bigger school. In his spanking new uniform, with his fine new satchel, Simon started at Big School. For a while everything seemed rosy.

But the bloom faded. Simon felt lost in so large a school. The pastoral arrangements had collapsed because his form master was ill and supply teachers were substituting. Heather found a sick note in the boy's pocket that should have been given in a week earlier. When she asked Simon about it, he said disconsolately that there'd been nobody to give it to anyway, 'Nobody noticed I wasn't there'. Heather went to see the Head and talked it through. He was concerned and kind. There would be a proper form teacher next term and meantime he would ensure that more care was taken of Simon's class.

There was more to it though. Simon simply felt overwhelmed in the place. Discipline was sketchy, and Simon found the uproar in corridors and classrooms hard to cope with. The formerly popular little boy became withdrawn and isolated. He increasingly invented ways to avoid school. The parents decided he must stay till the end of the first year when they would all review the situation.

Heather in particular blamed herself for not having foreseen this possibility, for having made quite the wrong decision. After all she was his mother. She told herself she should have realized that he would have been happier in a small, intimate environment. She felt guilty – felt she had failed her dear little sunshiny boy.

It took a long time for her to accept that she was not responsible for the outcome of her decision. Together with Alan, she had made the best possible decision open to them at the time. She could not and never would have been able to guarantee the outcome. The results of any decision or action are up to Providence. Human beings regrettably are not omnipotent. When she accepted that she was not responsible for anything other than trying her best, Heather began to be at peace with herself. This also rubbed off on Simon, who had sensed his mother's unhappiness and in turn felt *he* was the cause. When she overcame her personal crisis, he was better able to deal with his own problems.

This kind of dilemma recurs over and over with conscientious parents. Parents make hundreds of decisions every week – and some of them are bound to go awry. But too often we expect ourselves to make impeccable decisions with perfect conclusions – and clearly this is preposterous. Quite sane adults, who would accept the inevitable in their own lives, seem to think they should be invested with the power of the Almighty when it comes to their children.

The hidden agenda

Expectations are inevitable in the job of parenting. Sometimes our expectations sneak up on us unawares. A friend of mine, Susan, was a very relaxed parent of children born in the mid-sixties. Although she had been to university, her husband had not, and she was convinced that provided her son and daughter were happy and fulfilled, she would prefer them to be first class manual workers than mediocre professionals.

It was only when her son dropped out of his A-level year and announced he was going into a local garage to learn to work on bikes that she realized how much she had banked on her children automatically going on to university. She went through a bleak period, during which she was forced to take stock of her real expectations. She had to admit to herself that there was a lot of snobbery mixed up in her feelings and that she was disappointed in her son. Even understanding how she felt did not do away with her discomfort. She told him how she felt about his decision, admitting that she felt she'd 'failed' to motivate him and that he'd 'failed' to fulfil his academic potential. To her amazement he said, 'Oh no mum. You never gave me freedom to fail. You always expected me to be like you, to have the kind of achievements you had, the kind of goals you went for. I don't. I'm different. I want to learn about machines, I want to have my own business – and I don't need a university education for that.'

It was tough for Susan, mainly because she'd fooled herself for so long about her own real expectations. But our children always know. And sometimes it even looks as if they unerringly pick on the most sensitive spot with which to get at us. Teresa would certainly have said so. She and her husband Colin, good practising Roman Catholics, had invested everything in their brilliant only daughter Catherine. Cathy excelled in everything she did. She was always at the top of her form in school work, played the piano and oboe with distinction, and was no slouch on the hockey field. She was attractive and popular, and when she went to visit friends or to occasional parties, one or other of her parents would always fetch and carry her by car.

Cathy was 16 when her mother discovered contraceptive pills in the girl's coat pocket. Teresa was devastated, her dreams shattered. Despite all the effort she had put in to making sure her daughter had every opportunity to develop as a whole person with a secure career, Teresa's ultimate expectation for Cathy was for a beautiful white wedding in its full meaning. Cathy's academic and musical achievements were unimportant compared with the evidence of her loss of faith in her religion. Also, in Teresa's eyes, Cathy's accomplishments were mere frills to add to her value in the marriage market. Until that critical day when she saw the tell-tale little pills, she had not realized that Cathy did not share all her expectations. She felt betrayed, as though her daughter had stabbed her in the back, deliberately chosen the worst way to hurt her.

It is not a matter here of who was right or who was wrong. What is in question is the hidden agenda which many parents carry around – often hidden only from themselves. Cathy was quite aware of her mother's expectations. They just weren't her own. She loved her mother dearly, and did not want to hurt her, for which reason she had not discussed with her the painful reappraisal of her own religious position. It took several years before Teresa came to terms with her daughter's individual identity – her right to dream her own dreams and decide her own destiny.

We give away our expectations in small ways which are not lost on other people. Susan realized that she used to say to her boy, '*When* you go to university' – not '*If* you go to university'. She made assumptions. A lot of the time it is our job as parents to make assumptions. To assume that our children will keep their word, will turn up on time, will be honest. Stuff like that. But when we start making assumptions about their future, we can be in trouble. That, very definitely, is *not* our business.

It has occurred to me that adoptive parents may have less trouble with expectations than parents of the blood. It is just not possible to impose family traits, trends, and characteristics on an adopted child. There is constant surprise. When we can find our *own* children a constant surprise, and expect no qualities in them (bad or good) that we perceive in other members of the family, then we are in a good place, we are comfortable in our parenting job.

The self-fulfilling prophesy

Negative expectations are real black magic. And I have to say, most parents can catch themselves out in it.

Ever said, 'You ALWAYS do it wrong' ...? or 'You NEVER get it right' ...? Umm, thought so. Me too.

The sociological phrase is 'the self-fulfilling prophesy'.. If I keep telling my son that he *never* remembers to take his football boots upstairs however often I tell him, clearly he will have no reason to change my image of him. Since I consider him a slob, he'll be a slob. It's easier anyway to put up with a bit of nagging than to make the superhuman effort to lift a pair of football boots off the floor and labour upstairs with them.

There are endless variations of the 'You never–you always' kind – and they are all lousy tactics because they have the opposite effect to what they appear to be saying. 'That boy always gets it wrong'. Can you imagine talking like that in the office? It is the trade-mark of the nag – and quite a lot of fathers as well as mothers bear it. The person who says, 'You never' or 'You always' does not want a change for the better: they want to keep the status quo and a reason to complain. It is also a smart way of starting an endless, unprofitable argument.

Unprofitable because if you want those football boots taken upstairs – regularly – you have many options. You can confiscate them. Give them away. Throw them out. You can withold pocket money. Or food. Or treats. You can do fifty different things

– and *none* of them includes 'You always ' or 'You never'. You, after all, are the manager in your home. You keep the whole shoot running: your child does not. When your child gets to pay the mortgage and the bills, when they organize the food, the clothes, the furniture, the repairs and decorations, the drains, the festivals, the cleaning, cooking, mending, and provisioning, that's soon enough for them to decide what's what at home. They are not yet partners in the domestic enterprise.

In the meantime, you have one essential positive expectation. You expect to make the rules in your own home – and you expect your children to observe them.

Instinct and love

Instinct is not love

Biological power is frequently confused with love. It is not love. In its full true sense, love carries dimensions not only of protection and service but also of responsibility and justice. Love is not just an instinct, or even a feeling – it is a commitment to caring for the whole human potential of the other. To return to Donald and Fiona for a moment. When they gave in to their 'feelings' of parental protectiveness, and paid their son's bad debts over and over again, they did him a grave disservice. They only began to act in love when they stood back and gave the boy his inalienable right to experience the consequences of his own decisions. For them this was a much harder thing to do. It flew in the face of their 'instinctive' behaviour, and demanded an unaccustomed discipline. But discipline – self-discipline – is an essential ingredient of love. Love is not merely giving and forgiving. Love can also mean *not* giving.

Let us speak some more of love. The word will recur quite often as we go on, and it would be helpful to look carefully at what we mean when we use this battered little four-letter word.

We often hear about 'unconditional love'. One of my sons, in a teenage rage, roared at me, 'The trouble is you don't understand unconditional love. You only love me when I do things *your* way!' I was temporarily taken aback. Could he be right? It took me a while to realize that his accusation was false. I certainly did not always like – or approve – his behaviour. Equally certainly, I loved him. Unconditional love does not require unconditional approval. Love wants the best for the other. The best does not include bad behaviour.

Love may be selfish

Real love needs sometimes to be selfish. I do not love my children if I allow them to become predators, pillaging my personal time and space. Just because I am a parent, I do not have to be always and instantly available. I must mark out my private territory and gradually teach each growing child to respect it. Only thus can the child learn that love does not include dependence or tyranny. Far too many mothers (in particular) are conditioned to react like stricken beasts to a charge of selfishness. Their availability to the demands and requirements of everyone in the family is total. They stretch themselves on the altar of 'unselfishness' and await the ritual knife.

They do themselves and their family no favours. They teach their boy children to be dependent, demanding and tyrannical. They teach their girl children to be dependent, depersonalized victims in their own image.

It is no accident that the primary instinct in us all is self-preservation. It supercedes all others – and in the fully adult human, preservation of the self is preservation of the personality as well as the person. Mind you, it's dead easy to be supremely unselfish. If I give all my attention and emotional energy to my children (or my partner), thinking about them and worrying for them, I don't have time to do anything for or about myself. I don't have to worry about whether I can do anything, because I don't have to try. My children (and/or partner) will be doing it all for me. I can never, therefore be seen to fall or to fail. In a word, I cop out. That is definitely not on the parents' job description.

The good parent is a person *as well as* a parent.

Love is not possessive

Love is open, embracing others. It is not possessive, not exclusive. We all recognize possessive parents. The overprotective parents we talked about earlier were all, also, possessive people.

But there are other parents who less obviously entwine themselves into the fabric of their children's lives, so it is hard to see what is happening until it is too late. These are the parents whose subtle abuse of the biological instinct can damage or destroy either parent or child, and quite often both. Such a case was Madeleine and her daughter Imogen.

Madeleine's divorced mother died suddenly when Madeleine was 19. Bereft and alone, she met Terry, a man some years older than herself who offered a kindly shoulder to weep and lean on. Soon they were married. By the time Imogen was born a year later, the marriage was already shaky. They shared no interests, and neither of them knew how to explain their needs properly to the other. Terry, whose family had been stationed abroad throughout his childhood, had spent almost all his life in all-male institutions. From boarding school he went to public school, then into the army. He had only been in civilian life for two years when they met. Madeleine on the other hand, had had a very female-oriented upbringing. Her mother had never remarried. After some initial, unresolved rows, an icy silence settled between them. Their sex life petered out. Unable to communicate, too stiff-necked to ask for outside help, they became icily polite to one another, and Madeleine poured her frustration and bitterness, her love and energy, into the baby – *her* baby.

Terry had welcomed and wanted the baby. But Madeleine pushed him away, as she soon pushed everyone else away, so that only she, Madeleine, did everything for Imogen. Support, help, encouragements, treats, outings, holidays – all were provided, somehow or other, only by mummy. There was always a reason why Imogen couldn't go for a drive with daddy, or stay with cousins, or even accept a weekend in the country with school friends. Eventually Terry gave up. He spent more time out – often in the pub, returning slurred of speech, and seemingly impervious to the sighs of contempt, sneers, and tight-lipped silences. Soon Imogen too was firing well-aimed cracks at her father. When she was 16 her father left home to live with another woman.

But seemingly Imogen flourished. Madeleine encouraged her, helped with her homework, gave her endless time and attention. Not surprisingly, Imogen did well at school. She never went through a stroppy period, never had a bad school report, never got into trouble. She was a model daughter – and Madeleine basked in the admiration (and sometimes envy) of other, less apparently fortunate parents.

Imogen was a pretty girl, but never kept a boy friend long. Unlike most young girls, she didn't have any special girl friends either. Mummy was her best friend. After A-levels she won a place at university – but turned it down because she didn't feel ready to leave home yet. She decided to do a secretarial course locally, and found a good job with no difficulty. Eighteen months later, the firm opened a branch in Paris and asked Imogen to manage it on a much increased salary. She went to Paris – and stayed six weeks. Once again she came home to mummy.

At 25, Imogen was still living at home with mummy, still with no special friends of either sex. Then by chance she met an old schoolfriend who was lunching with her brother. Within two weeks Imogen had moved into his flat at the other end of London.

The effect on Madeleine was catastrophic. There had been no advance warning. One can see why, of course. Imogen had virtually no experience of defying her mother. It is all too probable that she felt she would never get away if she started to talk about it. She could only escape if it was sudden and irreversible. And of course she was right. Madeleine's personal resources were thin – her reason for living was inextricably bound up in her daughter. But 25 years of mutual dependence had built up such anger in Imogen that even a plea from her mother's doctor would not bring her home. Her anger had emerged suddenly, but it was deep and huge and engulfing. In fleeing from her mother, she felt that she was hauling her life out of the mouth of a devouring beast.

In the whole pattern of events, it is possible to see how deviously Madeleine's maternal instinct had masqueraded as love. Instead of helping her daughter grow into a whole person, she had insidiously kept her as dependent as a small child. Until her traumatic departure, Imogen had never been her *own* person: she was her mother's.

Madeleine was also suffering, because she had lived half her life in and through her daughter. She had made no life of her own. She had no career, no job, and no other relationships. Her whole attention had been focused on her daughter. But there is always a reckoning for those who refuse to live their own life. If our life is the first gift we are given on this earth, is not refusing to live it the original sin?

Self-sacrifice – the original sin

Now we come to the most difficult and hard-to-comprehend aspect of love. To love others we must first love ourselves. If I cannot care tenderly for this envelope of flesh, bones, brain, heart, spirit, and person which was entrusted to me at my birth, how can I know to care for another? If I have not first learnt to respect my own needs and requirements, how can I help another to respect their own – *and* mine?

It is strange in our society to talk about loving oneself. Never mind that one of the primary exhortations many of us heard was 'Love thy neighbour *as* thyself'. This, in some curious way has been transmuted into 'Love others *more* than thyself'. Particularly in the mythology of mothers, self-sacrifice has taken precedence over common sense.

Because we have not properly looked at what parenting is about, we have allowed a hidden agenda to grow up. On that hidden agenda, the concept of self-sacrifice figures large. But it is one thing to lay down your life for your child when the ship is sinking or the house is on fire. It is quite another to put your own needs at the bottom of the priority list in the ordinary business of everyday life.

It's also unworkable. It's a prescription for perfection and we are not here to spread 20 years of our living under the feet of our offspring. We are here to enjoy this earth – *together* with our children.

The hidden agenda of self-sacrifice is, as well as being unworkable, a nonsense. It presupposes that we can give to others something which we do not have ourselves. But if we do not have self-esteem and a good sense of self-worth (i.e. self-love) there is no way we can give these virtues to our children. If we are driven by guilt, resentment and anxiety, by fear, envy or despair, our children will absorb these and express them too.

The loving parent is not one who prodigally gives away his or her whole existence for a child: it is a parent who gives that child support from their own deep stock of strength and courage. If I want advice about my financial affairs, I go to the most successful financier I know. If I want help with my garden, I ask the friend whose garden flourishes. Our job as loving parents requires us not so much to *do* things for our children, but to *be* things for them.

LEGITIMATE POWER

'Legitimate power flows out of respect ... today parents have to earn respect. Because it is no longer an automatic right, it has become a duty. To do the job properly, respect is essential.'

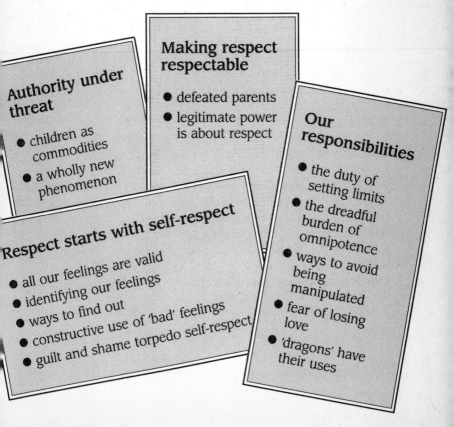

Authority under threat

- children as commodities
- a wholly new phenomenon

Making respect respectable

- defeated parents
- legitimate power is about respect

Our responsibilities

- the duty of setting limits
- the dreadful burden of omnipotence
- ways to avoid being manipulated
- fear of losing love
- 'dragons' have their uses

Respect starts with self-respect

- all our feelings are valid
- identifying our feelings
- ways to find out
- constructive use of 'bad' feelings
- guilt and shame torpedo self-respect

Authority under threat

It may surprise you to learn that parents have very little legitimate power over their children in the sense that legitimate means authorized by the law. In practice, of course parents hold most of the cards because they are the dispensers of everything a child needs to survive – food, shelter, protection and love.

But this is a total change. In all the long centuries which have gone before, children were in law and in practice the property of their parents – or more accurately, of their fathers if the child was born in wedlock. A man's children (like his wife) were regarded by society as his personal possessions and almost anything he did to them, short of murder, was considered to be his own affair. Church, state and society threw its whole weight behind the concept of paternal authority.

On the other hand, in a very real way society used to welcome children, and provide them with an instant and an honourable place. Children were an investment at every social level. Although many perished – (half the children born in 1831 died within their first five years) – more children were always needed, to work the land, to help with household industries, down the mines, in the factories, in the family business. In the upper echelons they were required to carry on the family name and affairs. Older children cared for younger ones and helped with tasks inside and outside the home. Since adults rarely lived to any great age, children could confidently be expected to care for their parents at the end. Children were thus endowed with social value from birth.

Today, lip service is paid (especially by some politicians) to 'the citizens of tomorrow'. But at grassroots children nowadays are regarded as a luxury or a liability – if not by individual parents, certainly by society at large. Now that life expectancy (for males) has gone up from 40 years in the 1840s to 71 in the 1980s a child would be a fairly risky insurance policy. Nor does one hear many new parents suggesting that the newborn will be a future asset in the office – or the dole queue.

Children as commodities

In this decade economists have taken to doing notional costings on children. One such valuation estimated that in 1983 the average cost of a child to the age of 18 was £80,000. An even more sophisticated analysis in *The Sunday Times* on 2 November 1986 went to the trouble of detailing the outlay, having regard to social class. By 1987, the Centre for Economic Policy Research had assessed the average loss of earnings for a mother of two to be £122,000.

This indicates a vast shift in public perception of children and of those who have them. The idea of children as commodities that somebody has to pay for is a far cry from the old view that they were intrinsically necessary and valuable for their potential contribution to the world. Today our children (and indirectly their parents) are furnished, not with social value, but with an in-built purposelessness and lack of responsibility in society.

Since children are widely regarded as a luxury it is difficult for parents to air problems – particularly problems of control. Society freely heaps burdens on parents, by raising the school leaving age or by reducing the chances for young people to get work and housing, but it offers little support in concrete terms. Meantime the value of children as consumers is exploited mercilessly. Asked if he felt our society welcomed children, a typical father replied, 'Children represent an enormous market. You only have to watch Saturday morning TV – the adverts are all geared to make children *want*, and manufacturers know parents are an easy touch. I'm not sure children are welcome, but they are seen as a potential market. If that's welcoming – yes!'

Sabotaged by Freud

Furthermore, parental authority has been seriously sabotaged by Freud. By the sixties, the ripples from the big stone he flung into the common pond had reached the farthest shore. His theories on the dire effects of parents had been sieved through the system and absorbed in common understanding. All parents – but particularly mothers – are commonly held to be somehow injurious to their young. This has become a 'received idea'. During the sixties and seventies parents might as well have worn labels round their necks, bearing the legend, 'Parents can seriously damage your mental health!' After having been in the right for centuries, parents were now, *de facto*, in the wrong. Mother-bashers thrived.

This attitude lingers on today. It accounts in part for the low self-esteem of parents, and for their feelings of inadequacy. Part and parcel of vulgar Freudianism is a kind of gloomy determinism. None of us (it would seem) can avoid being damaged by the things our parents do or don't do to us, feel or don't feel for us, and the same goes for our children. Growth, change and hope do not figure large. And of course, there is always the double-bind. If you don't feel that you are very damaged, or that your children are, you are kidding yourself. Your defence system must be working overtime. It is hardly surprising that in this social climate, parents feel vulnerable and demoralized.

Then there was Spock. He began auspiciously by addressing parents with the now-famous sentence: 'You know more than you think you do'. His *Baby and Child Care* published in 1955 was enthusiastically consulted by millions of parents, and talked about by more. The message that got through however, was 'Baby knows best'. This was translated into action in millions of homes, nurseries and playgroups. Babies who knew best grew into toddlers who knew best ... who grew into teenagers ...

The invention of the teenager

Ah yes. Teenagers. It is thought James Dean invented the term in 1956. Previously adolescents had neither a label nor any particular place in society. But in the early sixties, by virtue of labour shortages and their large disposable incomes, teenagers – as such – began to be courted by commerce and the media. They offered a prime market. They could be persuaded to buy clothes and cosmetics and music and cigarettes and confectionery and junk food. With the arrival of the teenaged consumer, coincidentally, built-in obsolescence was developed. But it didn't only apply to cars and refrigerators. It also applied to people. If not overnight, at least over a decade, the emphasis on the value of youth at the expense of age took over. A person over thirty was over the hill. Pressured from all parts of society, older people began to distrust their own values and to defer to those of the young. Only the young had answers.

The effect on parents was catastrophic. All their principles were up for grabs, many were demolished. The ease with which young people could find work made responsibility and discipline hard to engender. Thrift was laughed at. Waste was officially encouraged. The energy industries set about exhorting the public in commercials and advertisements to use more and more power. Obsolescence was more valued than durability – so the care of property and goods was actively discouraged. Craftsmanship gave way to plastic throwaways. Mending, repairing, saving, and making-do became things of the (very dead) past. Professor Marcuse validated the new philosophy and gave it academic weight. Timothy Leary, poet and scholar, threw away his books and became the new high priest of LSD. It became respectable to have no respect.

To top it all, we got the Pill. Oral contraceptives became available in the beginning of the sixties. Cures for gonorrhoea and syphilis had been found. Although abortion remained difficult to arrange for a further decade, most of the hazards of sex outside of marriage seemed to have been overcome. Within marriage, as never before, family size became a personal choice.

A wholly new phenomenon

Thus there came to pass a wholly new phenomenon in the history of the human race. Since time began people have honoured and respected their parents in gratitude for the very gift of life. Now could be heard a new voice: 'You chose to have me!' It did not take long for this to be followed by a corrosive corollary – 'So you owe me!' Do not mistake what I am saying. I do not mean to suggest that this is the attitude of any specific sons and daughters. It exists, nonetheless, as a very real undercurrent which needs to be taken into account.

Parents today have legal responsibilities rather than legal rights. As far as one can see, the only 'right' a parent really has is to prevent a child getting married before the age of 18, but even that can be overruled by a magistrate if the young person presents a reasonable case. Lord Denning, when he was Master of the Rolls, said, 'the legal right of the parent . . . starts with the right of control and ends with little more than advice.' (Quoted in *Children, Parents & the Law*, Consumers' Association, Which? Nov. 1985).

All this puts parents in a very different place from our predecessors. No longer is parental authority built into the job. Obedience does not happen 'because I say so'. Authority – *the legal right to make things happen* – is no longer supplied by the state.

Mercifully, the state does not have the last word. Legitimate power is otherwise dispensed – from a far older and more reliable source. Legitimate power flows out of respect. And that is very much our own private affair.

Making respect respectable

Parents who have good relations with their children, who are happy with their children's behaviour, speak of themselves as privileged – 'lucky'. They metaphorically keep their fingers crossed, looking over their shoulder against the dread spectres of law-breaking and drug use that might be lurking near.

Many parents talk plainly of their difficulties. Listen to Sally, mother of two boys aged 6 and 8: 'I feel my job is to give them correct guidance. It's not easy. They answer back. I wouldn't have dared talk to my parents like that. I don't know whether to chastise them *all* the time. I know they have to ask questions, but it's the way they do it – like "*Why* do I have to do it?" My mother was strict. Now I'm really glad of it. I regretted it at the time – when I was 16 years old I had to be in by 10 o'clock. She stuck by it. But I can't do it myself.'

Her husband Roger says: 'Rules? Decibels more like. We're just not sufficiently consistent. It depends on our own state of mind, how tired we are. Sometimes I'll say "OK". But if I've had a hard day it's, "Don't argue with me – IN!" maybe followed by a smack on the backside.'

Mr. P., a father with daughters of 20, 18, and 13 and a boy of 10 says: 'Sometimes they don't listen to you . . . I don't beat them, I tell them, talk to them. Sometimes it works, sometimes it doesn't. Outside influences are strong. When they were young they would listen . . . one time children used to do things willingly. Now parents have to give in.'

Brenda, a divorced parent of five children, their ages ranging from 7 to 20, agrees: 'Yes, it is hard to manage children. Harder as they get older. They backchat you. It's impossible sometimes. The bigger boys are sometimes even physically aggressive.'

Defeated parents

None of the parents say it, but all of them imply that their children lack respect. The children 'backchat', argue back, don't listen, get their own way. The parents are plainly uncomfortable, even unhappy about it, but in a curious way they are spiritless, defeated.

What are we to make of this? These particular parents are typical of thousands upon thousands of middle class mothers and fathers, living in quiet, law-abiding areas in our towns and cities. In some areas and in some homes it is far more serious – when the children are involved with drugs or law-breakers. But these mothers and fathers are symptomatic of a parental paralysis which appears to be replicated all over the country. It shows not only in homes but in schools. A poll commissioned by the National Union of Teachers reported in June 1988 that one in five teachers reported incidents of violence against teachers, one in 14 had been assaulted or threatened, 80 per cent reported verbal abuse. The poll covered teachers from all kinds of schools, state and independent alike.

Legitimate power is about respect

We have to swallow the fact that the old reverence for parents – just because they *are* parents – is not going to come back. For centuries children were forced to go along with parental dictatorship and hypocrisy. It won't wash today. With it has gone strict discipline – 'instant obedience'. On the other hand, permissiveness, as commonly understood and practised in the two post-sixties decades, does not seem to be a roaring success either.

Yet as long a humans continue to want babies and babies continue to need parents, the imperative for legitimate power will remain. Reduced to its simplest –

Legitimate power is about respect. All children have a deep and enduring need to respect their parents.

It is integral to their sense of security and self-worth, and we ignore this at our peril. The requirement to honour and respect our parents is an essential oil which lubricates all social relations. It permeates every society and every theological tradition. It is basic to the human condition.

Respect for their parents is not only important to children. It is vital for parents too. To do their job properly, parents need to command respect. It is simply not good enough to sigh about 'children these days'. Children these days are no different from how they've ever been. The difference lies not in children but in society – of which we are all a part – and the fact that a lot of parents have mislaid their own personal capacity to create respect.

Being a parent today is certainly challenging. When respect was built in to the job, parents could get away with temper tantrums and sulks, and hypocritical rules ('Do as I say, not what I do') – and take their unresolved personal conflicts to the grave. They would still receive lip service respect from their children. Not so today.

Today parents have to earn respect. Because it is no longer an automatic right, it has become a duty. To do the job properly, respect is essential. Our children's respect – but first of all, our own.

Respect starts with self-respect

First we have to be clear that unless we have self-respect in good measure, nobody else is going to respect us. Also remember that we can give our children nothing that we do not have ourselves. Let us look at what self-respect in your job actually means. In practice it boils down to being comfortable in your work, feeling good about it. You accept with equal ease your duties and responsibilities, your rights and your privileges.

Self-respect involves self-control. This does not mean the buttoned-up, tight-lipped rigidity and repression of feelings that previous generations apparently understood it to be. Here we find another great change in society. Until recently, people did not talk about their feelings even in the bosom of the family. One's feelings were one's own business and it was either bad form, or self-indulgent, or both, to talk about them. If you hurt, you hurt in secret. If you suffered feelings of anger or despair or envy, you might confide them to your diary or your prayers but most probably you would contain them in silence. The aim was to keep the lid on.

So tightly was the lid kept on that many people – possibly most people – came to believe it was wrong even to feel angry, afraid or jealous. Many of us learnt early to sit in judgement on our emotions and often tried to convince ourselves we do not have these 'bad' feelings. The only feelings permitted in many families were the good feelings – happiness, gratitude and such like.

All our feelings are valid

Rubbish, of course. We all feel angry, afraid, depressed, disappointed, jealous, envious and greedy – from time to time. These feelings are not only natural, they are necessary to our survival as individuals and as a species. They have a place in our lives. We need fear to generate adrenalin and courage, we need anger and disappointment to stimulate action in unfavourable circumstances. We need envy, even a little greed, to encourage initiative and achievement.

And therein lies the dilemma. Our feelings are a human and (possibly) inevitable response to a situation; our task as parents is to choose the appropriate action to use them to enhance our personal self-respect. We need to find ways of dealing creatively and usefully with our feelings.

We have Freud and his successors to thank for recognizing the way we all bury and distort our feelings. Their insights into the consequences of repression opened up a whole new can of worms. We now recognize that unacknowledged negative feelings can do much harm. Truly this is the enemy within. If you know or suspect you have a serious problem, don't be too proud (or pig-headed) to get professional help. At some time or other, everyone needs some help. There's no disgrace. Better to ask for help now than to have it thrust upon you later.

Sonia is a classic example. She sought professional help because she was deeply worried about her occasional bursts of ungovernable rage towards her dearly loved son Toby, then aged five. Sonia, whose mother had died when she was very young, had been brought up entirely by her father to whom she was devoted. He was a man of great charm and distinction. But as she talked in the safety and calm of the therapist's rooms, she found herself recalling and recounting long-buried incidents which had occurred in her early life. Painfully she recovered memories of her younger self – a self who had hated her father because of his cruelty to her mother. Although he was always kind to Sonia, her father had had no affection for his wife. One black day when Sonia was five she had overheard a row between them – her father shouting that her mother was stupid, useless, and good for nothing but her money, her mother sobbing and moaning noisily. After her father slammed out, Sonia had tried to comfort her mother, appalled to see her so stricken. 'He'd like me to die, why can't I die?' Less than a year later, her mother did die. She had had an undetected cancer and the end was swift. In the child's mind, her father had somehow made it happen.

As she talked about it, 20 years later, her rage at her father began to surface, rage which as a little girl she had been too fearful to express. She had seen, she thought, the results of anger. She dared not risk expressing her own anger in case her father died too. She loved and hated him, feared him and feared for him, because of the fury she felt towards him.

Gradually the connection with Toby became clear to her. Toby greatly resembled his grandfather. Sonia had always seen this of course, but she had not realized the connection had also been made in her unconscious mind. The undealt-with anger at her father was hooked unpredictably to occasional expressions or gestures the little boy unwittingly made. Old memories triggered explosions of pain inside her. In the therapist's room, she felt safe to express her grief and fear and rage, and so she was gradually enabled to defuse the feelings. They no longer rose unbidden to threaten her innocent little son. She recovered control over her emotions – and with it, her self-respect began to return.

Identifying our feelings

We have to recognize our feelings for what they are but sometimes because of shame or old habit, we do not readily identify them. Quite often they wrap themselves in a sort of shroud of discomfort.

There are several useful techniques for getting your real feelings out into the open. Is there a situation, or a person that makes you feel uncomfortable? Something that your mind shies away from like a nervous horse? Keep your attention tethered to it, really look at the situation. What is it that bugs you? If you are being quite honest, I guarantee you will find it concerns some aspect of yourself that you are not particularly proud of.

To illustrate this I will tell you a story of two families, whose children were close friends. John and Jean had two little boys; Henry and Rebecca had a girl and two boys. For three years the two families were friends – the four boys in and out of each others' houses after school and all through the holidays. John was marvellous with them and often at week-ends took all four boys on expeditions – walking, climbing, fishing, or just throwing a ball about. This was particularly good for the children of Henry and Rebecca because Henry was immersed in his law practice and spent most week-ends working. Then one summer a local political issue drove a wedge through the two sets of parents. It was not resolved, and by chance the break coincided with John and Jean deciding to move permanently into the country. The rift became permanent, now that the children were also physically separated.

Four years later, Rebecca and Henry learnt that John had died. Rebecca knew she ought to get in touch with Jean – either by telephone or letter, but she balked. She kept putting it off and putting it off. Finally she forced herself to look at the whole situation. She sat down and started writing out what she *really* felt. She could hardly remember the details of the final row with Jean which had precipitated the break, but she did remember the heat of their argument. A heat disproportionate to the subject, fuelled, she suddenly realized, by her previously unacknowledged envy for Jean's husband. John was exactly the sort of father she would have liked her own children to have. She did not want him as a husband (she thought him nice but dull) – but as a father he was admirable. Much of this she was able to write in a letter to Jean, and her own relief was tremendous. Being able to admit to herself (and even to someone else) that she had had damaging negative feelings curiously dispelled them. When she thought of the other family now, she could think of them with warmth, compassion, and real affection. Her own devils vanished once they were exposed to the light.

Ways to find out

Rebecca's method is effective and easy. It meant forcing herself to scrutinize her behaviour and motives. She wrote down the whole incident – as pitilessly as she could. I do not know why writing it down should be so successful, but it is. In some odd way, our inner honesty seems to take a hand. When you write down the whole story, hidden bits of the truth seem to sneak in. When you come to read it afterwards – preferably not immediately, but a few days later – your own part in it usually becomes clear.

I first did this years ago, because a distant connection of my family who had made great demands on me, and who had always behaved shabbily, threatened another visit. I hated the thought. I kept thinking about all I'd done for her and how ungratefully she had acted, simply demanding more and more from me. So I wrote it all down – from my first meeting with her until her last tele-phone call. What a nasty surprise I got! Sure she'd behaved badly. The catalogue of her misdeeds was plain to see. What I hadn't expected was to discover how unpleasantly I had behaved myself. I had set myself up for everything she dished out. I hadn't really treated her as a human or my equal. I had been arrogant, snobbish, and unkind. Discovering these unlovely character traits in myself actually enabled me to feel better – because there was something I could do about it. When it was 'all her fault', I was impotent (and furious). When I accepted my own part in it, I had the power to change the situation. I could behave differently. (For the record, I shall tell you the outcome. I put off her impending visit, giving myself time to come to terms with my discoveries and to work through my feelings, then invited her a few months later. Without even trying, I must have spoken and acted quite dif-ferently to her. She arrived with flowers! – and behaved in a friendly and pleasant way throughout the visit. Over time, we became good friends until her death two years ago.)

Another way of ferreting out nasties is to listen to your own words. If you hear yourself saying (without prompting), 'I'm not angry, I'm only ...' think about it. You probably are very angry indeed. Who said anything about anger anyway? *You* did.

If you find yourself feeling unaccountably grey one morning, and cannot blame the weather or your state of health, think about what may have set it off. A haunting scent? A task you have to do? Something someone said last night that you laughed off? Don't just brush it aside – look for it, and having found it, look *at* it.

Now this is not just self-indulgent introspection. If you don't acknowledge the negative feelings (which are not unique to you) they will fester inside, and explode at inconvenient or inappro-priate moments. It is not possible to have self-control if you don't know what you're supposed to be controlling. So take your courage and look at it. I suggested it could be easy. It often is. I did not say it was painless. It isn't.

Constructive use of 'bad' feelings

The whole purpose of all this is to emphasize the fact that we cannot help having some of our feelings – but we *can* help how we express them. If the gas company has messed me about, and

I have let myself become angry, I can take it out on my family, my china, or myself. Alternatively, I can do something constructive like writing a heated letter to the head of the gas company and making sure the local office gets a reprimand. That certainly is a more adult and appropriate way of using my anger than kicking the cat, and it's a good deal more satisfying.

Our feelings are our own. Nobody can *make* us feel anything, any more than someone can make us believe or think anything. Also, we do not *have* to retain our feelings any longer than we choose to. We can choose to hang on to our anger or our disappointment or our fear – or we can look at it, do something (adult) about it, and let it go.

Guilt and shame torpedo self-respect

Self-respect does not survive in the company of guilt or shame. A fortunate few appear to know by instinct (or maybe from their own parents' example) how to handle these two difficult emotions, but most of us aren't given many sensible guidelines. 'They threw away the lesson-book when I came along' said a friend ruefully. Many of us understand exactly what he meant.

But there *are* ways of handling guilt and shame – and we can learn about them and begin to practise them. The process can be quite painful, exercising muscles you didn't know you had, but the benefits, in comfort and well-being, and restoration of self-respect, are remarkable.

Let's first establish what we're talking about. *Guilt* refers to actions: lying, cheating, malicious gossip, stealing, assaulting your children or condoning cruelty towards them – these are all actions which make us feel guilty. *Shame* is different. Whereas guilt is concerned with things we have done, shame is concerned with what we are – or are not. While guilt refers to the breaking of rules, shame is about not meeting expectations – our own, or other people's (real or supposed). We feel shame because we are not a good enough parent, or because we were not able to keep a marriage together, because we are poor, or unsuccessful in business, because a relative has acted deviantly (or *we* did in the past). Shame involves our dignity, not our conscience. In the general way, shame touches the raw nerve of our impotence – because almost always it involves circumstances over which we have no control at all.

Dealing with guilt

Let's first take guilt – the bitter fruit of conscience. Conscience is not something we hear much about these days. Like antimacassars and aspidistras, like samplers and snuff, one might suppose it to be extinct. Not so. Your conscience (and mine) is alive and kicking. Being kicked by conscience is an all too common experience. What we don't always know is how to deal with it.

Our aim, as responsible parents, is to arrange our lives to maximize our internal comfort. Hence it is necessary to begin by admitting any and every action we feel guilty about – at least to ourselves. This gets us halfway there. Bringing our guilty secrets up into the air takes much of the poison out of them – however dark or disgusting they may be.

Then we need to consider what we can do. Since action has been the cause of guilt, action is needed to resolve our guilt. Can we make amends? Repair the damage? Put matters right? However, if we have harmed somebody else, would disclosure do even more harm? To settle my conscience by causing pain to someone else is *not* making amends. It is making things worse.

There are two important stages here: one is admission of our own wrong doing, and the second is being *willing* to put it right. It may be that the opportunity to make amends has not yet arisen, but just being prepared to do so brings extraordinary relief.

Often we have done bad things to people who have also done bad things to us. This can raise problems. Not, I hasten to add, insurmountable problems. Action is still necessary. You are at this point concerned only to clear *your* side of the street, making *yourself* comfortable. Another person's bad behaviour is their problem – they have to live with it, not you. You only have to live with *your* conscience – and your aim, we hope, is to have it nicely spring-cleaned. So just for the moment, put aside their bad behaviour, and think about your own. Rebecca, who had difficulty writing her condolence letter, was a good example of this. Jean and John *had* behaved badly over that political issue, and had also, Rebecca believed, instigated the final row. But it was only when she firmly put aside what they had done and rigorously searched her own conscience, that she found it was her own unworthy feelings (envy) that were really bugging her. This discovery enabled her to feel comfortable, to act constructively, and to mend an unnecessary breach in a friendship.

'Conscience doth make cowards of us all'. It also doth make us bad-tempered, irritable, and a pain to live with. It causes us to blame others for the very things we ourselves are guilty of. It makes us torture ourselves with justifications when a plain admission of error would simplify our day. Frequently we behave worse towards people we have hurt – hating them for the damage we have done them. All this negative stuff inside us is lethal. It grows out of undealt-with guilt. In our own interests as going human concerns – and in particular as responsible parents – we need to attend to the promptings of that not-so-quaint anachronism, our conscience. You may need all your courage, almost certainly you will have some pain – but the long-term benefits are invaluable. It's the very best kind of massage for your ego.

Dealing with shame

Shame is very frequently concerned with matters on which other people have opinions. Since people have opinions on just about everything, we can choose to feel shame about anything at all.

Evelyn is no stranger to shame. She is a single parent and also a responsible, sensible mother who runs her own word-processing agency from home. Her daughter Harriet is therefore no latch-key child. Harriet was an easy, responsive little girl, but at 13, like many other adolescents, she went through a difficult patch. She became uncooperative: unwilling to do her homework, tidy her room or help with any household chores. At school she became friends with a small group of girls who took occasional afternoons off to drift round the town centre – shoplifting. On the third occasion that Harriet went with them, the group was caught. The wrath of school and law fell on their heads. Evelyn was appalled.

By good fortune no one insisted on the girls being charged. Restitution and apologies were promised and delivered, and that should have been the official end of the matter. But the authorities' view was that having no visible father, Harriet must be the ring-leader. The other three girls each could show a proper pair of parents. More interest was taken in Harriet than in the others. Her class teacher made a special arrangement to discuss her progress at school once a month. The local policeman called at the house for a friendly, informal chat. It was all well-meaning, but it was also quite shaming in Evelyn's view, because the other girls did not get the same treatment, and because she was convinced (rightly as it turned out) that Harriet had learnt her lesson and was genuinely contrite about her actions and behaviour.

Evelyn couldn't let the matter rest. She felt uncomfortable because 'the authorities' had made clear their concern about Harriet's lack of a father. She felt ashamed that she had failed her daughter. It was irrelevant that the father had done the deserting. In popular psychology she was to blame for choosing him in the first place. Thus she cleverly boxed herself into Catch 22.

It was one of Harriet's new friends, Marion, who inadvertently helped her out. When the girls' trouble had come out, Marion's parents had a huge row – the latest in a long line of arguments. The father blamed the mother for being weak, the mother complained the father was never home. The row had escalated. The parents now slept in separate rooms and talked about divorce, when they spoke at all. Marion came round to visit Harriet. At tea, she said sadly, 'I do envy you Harriet. It's so peaceful here – you never have scenes. I love both my parents, but they're horrid to each other. I wish they'd stop fighting.'

Evelyn's shame melted. She realized how useless it had been to agonize over a past that could not be changed. She had not been able to provide the statutory two-parent nuclear family for her daughter, but the responsibility for that was by no means only hers. She had, at any rate, provided a peaceful and loving home for Harriet. All this she had known in her head but now she accepted it at a deeper level.

You will notice that I suggested we could choose whether or not to feel shame. By and large that's so. That's a fundamental difference between guilt and shame. Harriet did have cause to feel guilt. She had stolen, and guilt was an inevitable consequence. But Evelyn's *shame* was about something she had no control over. She could not bring back her husband. She did, however, have a choice about whether or not she was going to give herself a hard time for being a single parent.

Your best is good enough

It is said that you can walk up to anybody in the street and whisper meaningly, 'I know your secret' – and they'll instantly look alarmed. The test is not 100 per cent guaranteed, but certainly most people have something in their lives that they'd rather not disclose in public. Don't make a meal of your own shame if you are doing the best you can today.

On the question of shame it is important to ask yourself seriously if you can do anything about the situation. Would you even want to do anything? If not, then accept it for what it is – a fact of life, as much a part of your destiny (and your child's) as the place in which you were born and the colour of your eyes. If you are a loving parent, you are already giving your child other tremendous gifts of mind and spirit, and who ever promised that the world was fair?

Shame must be faced

If your shame is concerned with past behaviour of your own, be kind to yourself. In her extreme youth, Maria had sold her sexual favours for money. Not to put too fine a point on it, she had been a prostitute between the ages of 15 and 17. The events which led her to this course of action are not material here. Suffice that she was certainly an unwilling victim of circumstances. Resilient and resourceful, she fought her way into mainstream life and put her past behind her. Twenty-five years later, happily and faithfully married, she had not fully come to terms with the secret burden of her ancient shame. This caused her to treat her two teenage daughters with extreme strictness – and when the elder threatened high rebellion, Maria had to come to terms with her shame – or risk the loss of her daughter. Resourceful as ever, she sought out a family counsellor and talked out her history, her pain, and her shame. She came to terms with her own past and was helped even to acknowledge that she was far from being the loser she had labelled herself.

Shame must be faced, or it will gnaw away your vitals. If it is very deep and embedded, you may need to take time. Trust your inner self, pay attention to your feelings, and in time you will find strength and courage to confront your problem. Maybe you will find it necessary to ask for some short-term professional help. There's a lot of it about. Just keep your ears open.

The key is control. I can learn to control how I act today. I can decide today how I shall speak, think, and behave. I have no control over yesterday. If I have done everything possible to put right the bad things I did hitherto, and if I intend *today* not to repeat them, then I have the right to hold my head high.

Half the time we set ourselves up. We (figuratively) creep around, inviting adverse comment on the very thing we dread.

When we face the problem internally, seeing it for what it is, we can then decide to face the world open and unafraid. At the start we may have to 'fake it to make it' – pretending to an assurance we don't have. But provided our own conscience is comfortable, we can win.

Find courage

To deal with both guilt and shame we have to find courage.

For guilt we need courage to admit we are wrong. For shame, we need courage to accept that we are *all right*.

With all our warts and imperfections, we are today just as we were meant to be. Shame tells us slyly that we are not good enough. If we are doing our best – *today*, that is quite good enough.

Most single parents have plenty of opportunities to feel shame – if they choose. But parents in pairs are also vulnerable. Perhaps a child wasn't very much wanted? Perhaps you were going through a bad patch with your partner when the child was on the way? Well we have recently been informed that babies record everything that goes on round them while they are in the womb. Woe unto you! What did you do to your hapless baby before it was born? Or did you go into hospital when your child was small – leaving it with someone else? What maternal deprivation did you cause? Have you set the scene for a future delinquent? Or did you, because of your job requirements, spend months last year away from home? Do you realize that children's achievements are (probably) directly related to paternal interest and input?

See what I mean? Shame can sneak in through a hundred side doors, especially when there's a crisis or a difficulty. Mostly it can be conquered by facing it. If there's nothing you can actually do about the situation, then accept it as a fact of your life and your destiny.

Prisoners of conscience

It is vital to be vigilant about both guilt and shame for the very good reason that family management requires that you, as a parent measure up. You don't need a halo, but you do need to be able to look the world (and your children) in the eye. You can't do this if unresolved guilt or shame are your secret companions.

Shame sends our self-respect plummeting. And when we are guilty we bluster, we don't meet people's eyes, we explode unexpectedly, we avoid certain people and situations.

We can kid ourselves that we're getting away with it. Maybe we even get away with the facts. We *do not get away from our own conscience*. Like it or not, we are its prisoners. Our chains rattle in the long corridors of the mind, and those who are near and dear to us will hear the muffled echoes in the words we have said, and in other words we have not said. There is no escape but through our own actions. To measure up we have to deal first with ourselves. We have to put our own internal house in order.

As we build up our self-respect, remarkable changes automatically happen in all our relationships. Because we act and speak from a position of internal strength, we act and speak with a new and unassailable authority. We command respect, because our self-respect is built upon bedrock. The respect we have earned is infinitely more valuable and enduring than any number of legal rights. It is the basis of legitimate power, older by far than history itself.

Our responsibilities

As we have seen, the wheel has turned. In Victorian times, parents had many legal rights, few responsibilities. Parents today have hardly any legal rights and rather more responsibilities, lasting longer because of extended compulsory education. In fact, whether legally required or not, parents have always accepted that responsibility is the name of the game.

Responsibility embraces much more than provision of hearth and home. It is written into the job description that parents make the rules – and make them stick. To be sure, many of the rules handed down to us from the past are no longer appropriate today. But many children these days are allowed to make their own rules – or dispense with them entirely. When that happens nobody wins.

Let's look again at what Sally said: 'My mother was strict. Now I'm really glad of it. I regretted it at the time – when I was 16 years old I had to be in by 10 o'clock. She stuck to it. But I can't do it myself.'

What Sally is really saying is that she is not as good a mother as her own mother was. She knows her mother's 'strictness' was valuable – but she is unable (unwilling?) to do the same for her own children.

Sally is not unique. She is like hundreds, or thousands, of parents who admit they let their kids get away with it – whatever 'it' may be. These parents are uncomfortable because they feel they are not doing their job properly.

The duty of setting limits

I'm not talking about the specific question of whether a 16 year old should or shouldn't be in by 10 o'clock. That depends on the circumstances and the individual parent's decision. I am assuming the parent made the most loving decision. If it's unpopular – tough. We are not in the business of winning popularity polls. We are in the business of being good parents.

One of the less helpful legacies from the permissive era is the woolly idea that parents should try to keep children always happy. This is often translated as not crossing them. To get their own way children can demonstrate unsuspected powers of single-minded persistence. They will perform miracles of lateral thinking. They have been known to raise nagging to an art-form. And of course, the work of testing parents to the limit is an essential part of their development. They need to establish exactly what they can get away with.

It is equally vital that they should be brought up short *when you decide*. It is *their* aim to find out, *your* task to show them – in practice – what is permissible and what is not.

The dreadful burden of omnipotence

All of us spend a great deal of our lives trying to make sense of the world, trying to bring order out of the chaos of impressions, stimuli, and sensations which bombard us from all sides from the moment we leave the womb. In infancy and childhood, it is almost a full-time occupation. For this reason, parents who do not set limits for their children – and stick to them – give the child a dreadful burden. I do not say that lightly. If there are no limits to a child's power, how can the child cope with the appalling responsibility? It is left with nothing less than omnipotence. Mother and father are the only people of real consequence in a child's world. If they can be controlled by the child, the whole infinite, terrifying universe must be the child's to control. Do you really want to do *that* to your son or daughter?

If you do not give your child the security of limits, you are doing the child a serious disservice. If you let a Terrible Two rule the roost with tantrums and tears, if you let a manipulative teenager make all his or her own rules and regulations, you are giving short change on the job.

Maeve and Michael had an enchanting, thriving baby boy called

Sean. Sean had discovered very early in life (at about 9 months) that he could cry himself sick when he wanted to. Surprisingly, he only did this in the evenings when, having been bathed and fed and sung to and kissed goodnight, he was tucked into his cot. Maeve and Michael took it in turns to pick the little one up, wash and change him and, after checking his temperature and giving him a good cuddle, put him back to bed. He would then give a repeat performance. In time they found it easier just to keep him with them all night. He continued to thrive – but whenever the parents tried to return him to his cot, he threw up. Then Maeve became pregnant again. Her doctor – who had been unable to help hitherto – finally gave her an appointment with a paediatrician in a big teaching hospital. Maeve felt rather silly, as she brought in her beautiful healthy baby, now aged 15 months, and told the doctor about her problem. She ended, 'I would leave him if he only cried, but naturally I can't leave him lying covered in sick, can I?'

'Can't you?' asked the doctor, conversationally. There was a long pause while Maeve digested this. Then the doctor continued, 'Who runs your house? You and your husband – or the baby?'

That evening Sean was bathed and fed and sung to and kissed and put to bed in his cot. Feeling she had the support of the whole medical profession behind her, Maeve said firmly to the small child who lay innocently clutching his bear, 'Now tonight nobody is coming in to you. Sleep well darling – and I'll see you in the morning.' She turned out the light, closed the door, and waited for the wail of protest.

Nothing happened. For the first time in six months, their evening and night was undisturbed by the roar of outraged (and vomit-covered) infant. He never tried it on again. Maeve said she can only conclude that the baby knew by the *way* she spoke – he couldn't have understood the actual words. Knowing she was doing the right thing, she spoke with the voice of authority – and even at 15 months, Sean recognized it. From this small, undramatic (if tiring) episode, Maeve learnt an invaluable lesson. As her family grew, in size and age, she was to face many trials of strength between herself and her children. Never again did she flabbily collapse as she had done with the baby Sean. She now knew that she could make the rules and make them work.

Although parents dislike children getting their own way, children dislike it too. In the short term, they may be pleased with themselves for winning permission to play in the park or for getting the brilliant new bike. But at another, deeper level there is no long-term satisfaction in knowing your parents are a pushover.

Parents have no business being a pushover. It's not what parents are for, and nobody knows it better than your child.

Ways to avoid being manipulated

First it is important to give yourself time. In the hurly burly of life with children, a parent sometimes gets stampeded into snap decisions. 'When are we going to have tea?' 'May I go and play with Lucy?' 'Can I take the dog for a walk?' 'Jamie's taken my jacket – make him give it back!' 'I don't *want* to go to Auntie June's on Saturday – why do I have to?' 'Why can't I go to play with Lucy?' 'Can I wear my new jeans?' 'Can I have a new bike?' — In the cross-fire, it's possible to forget the magic words: 'I'll think about it.'

Thinking about it means just that. OK, you don't want to give the child a new bike. You need to know your reasons – *for your own sake*, not theirs. You are facing a wily negotiator. Be clear in your own head. Is it because the old bike still has a lot of mileage in it? Or you cannot really afford a new one? Are you afraid about the child's safety? Is it a character matter – the child has not looked after the old bike properly? There may be other reasons: dig them out and get your own mind straight.

Then decide whether or not to give your child reasons. You may decide not to give a reason. And *you are perfectly within your rights to give no reason*. Few parents today realize this. You do *not* have to give your child a reason for all your decisions. It is quite legitimate to say, 'I have thought about getting you a new bike, and I've decided the answer is no.' If pressed, the only further remark you need to proffer is, 'I do not wish to.'

This may appear old-fashioned, even unfriendly. It is neither. Until your child is an adult, able to pull their weight and pay their way in the full sense of the word, they are *not* entitled to reasons. You are the provider of all goods and services, and you do not have to justify your decisions. Furthermore, experience will probably remind you that if you lay yourself open to argument, you can easily be manœuvred or charmed into changing your mind. Promises will be made of Herculean help around the house, of Saturday jobs, and amazing school results. Naturally this bike is far, *far* safer than the other old banger which is positively *lethal*. Friends will be dragged into the argument. You will discover that all the most admirable children have this new kind of bike or are about to get it. How can you possibly refuse?

Well, you can. And in the business of parenting, sticking to your decision is the most friendly gesture you can make. It won't be possible all the time – but if you start using tactics that avoid confrontations, you are already winning. What is more, this procedure has a secondary payoff. Children are not stupid. When nagging is discovered to be unproductive, nagging will ease off.

I am not recommending edicts from on high as the only way of negotiating. What I am saying is that in some circumstances edicts from on high are the best course. Children do not need their egos massaged by being party to all decisions.

If you believe it is dangerous for the child to go to the park without adult supervision, you will doubtless say so. But if you believe your child needs plenty of sleep, then bedtime at seven (or eight or nine) is a fact of the child's life – not *necessarily* an issue to be discussed. If you don't have the money for a posh new bike with knobs on, then engaging in a discussion about it with a child is not going to produce it. It all depends on what *you* want to do.

And sometimes it is important that children understand their position in the scheme of things. Their position is that they are at the receiving end of a great deal of parental love, care, attention, kindness, thought, food, shelter, protection, and support. They can accept – without questioning – a few knocks along with the good stuff. In the scheme of things they need to learn that parents set the limits.

I'd love to leave it there, letting you move on to the next section in a glow of righteous self-approval, but there are two other matters which we need to explore.

Fear of losing love

How often do you let your child get away with things because you fear their disapproval? Because you can't bear to see that little face crumpling up in disappointment? Because you get such pleasure from pleasing? Because your child might – even briefly – stop *loving* you if you refuse? Does this apply to you? Is this something you need to think about?

Then again, many parents, for all sorts of personal reasons, find it very hard to refuse even quite improper requests. I have met several parents who have done without holidays so that their children could join school groups to far-flung places. I don't mean field trips. I mean those jaunts abroad in school groups. I'm not saying these are necessarily without value. But parents who give expensive treats which may have only minimal educational value to their children *at real cost to themselves* are not doing themselves or their children any favours. The child may be disappointed at quite a different, longer-lasting level.

Despite all their nagging, children care desperately about their parents. They know when parents are weary, overworked or straining to make ends meet. But by the nature of things, they are impotent to 'make it better'. They are also inexperienced in setting priorities for themselves. That is the parents' job. If we allow our children to add unnecessary pressure to our lives we really lay the potential for guilt on them. Of course they want to go on the trip with their friends. But when 'yes' means a heavy parental sacrifice, an unequivocal 'no' can be a kindness. Of course they'll try it on. Honour demands it. But it is the parents' responsibility to take the long view – and the right decision.

Dragons have their uses

'Dragon' parents are sometimes worth their weight in gold. Peer pressure on children can be as difficult for the youngster as it is for the luckless parent at the next remove. Youngsters can be persuaded to beg for things which they know are bad, dangerous, or unnecessary. An unyielding parent can be a tremendous help in this quite commonplace situation. The 'dragon' parent can provide an unassailable reason for not doing, acquiring, or attending whatever is in question. Most children have an almost obsessive need to save face in front of their peers. It's in your gift to do the right thing – and maybe you'll be (secretly) a godsend. Don't overlook it.

If you feel in your guts that you don't want to permit something, just say no. After all, you can't be right all the time, but your parental antennae are worth their weight in gold. Your child may loathe you for a good ten minutes, but that's no cause for dismay. I bet you've been fed up with him or her for a good 20 minutes before now. It is not the end of the world. What is important is to remember the long-term priorities of parenting.

As I said before, love is not just giving. It can be not giving. Refusing a request may be the most loving thing you can do for your child. If you know both in your head and your heart that what you have decided is right, don't mess about. Stick with it. Your child may be miffed and think you are an old stick-in-the-mud – and that's just too bad. You are not their brother or sister. You are the parent – and that's the best thing you can be for your child.

Has it ever occurred to you to wonder why the drugs message, 'Just say no' has been so memorable? Is it because many parents have forgotten to teach their children – *by example* – how to say 'no' and make it stick?

When our children ask to have or to do things because their friends have or do them we should remember that all the other children are giving their parents exactly the same message. Peer pressure is not a myth, but you don't have to bow to it unless you choose to. The buck stops with you. Peers are no substitute for parents.

When we take full responsibility for setting realistic limits for our children, we reap the full benefit of legitimate power. It isn't just the children who benefit. It's ourselves. Parenting is a great deal smoother, infinitely more comfortable and effective, when we have the use of legitimate power – from within.

DYNASTIC POWER

'in the end the proper use of dynastic power boils down to this: what will most help your children to fulfill their whole potential? . . .
dynastic power is also about handing on our skills and knowledge and wisdom to our children . . .'

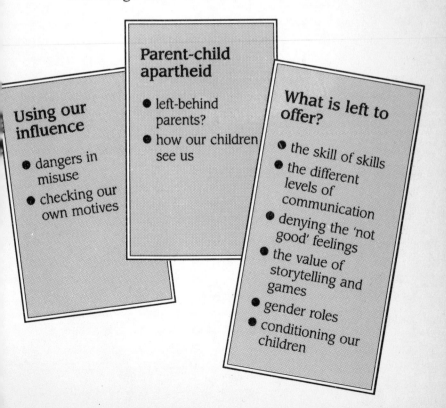

Using our influence

- dangers in misuse
- checking our own motives

Parent-child apartheid

- left-behind parents?
- how our children see us

What is left to offer?

- the skill of skills
- the different levels of communication
- denying the 'not good' feelings
- the value of storytelling and games
- gender roles
- conditioning our children

Using our influence

Dynastic power is not confined to royalty, nobility, and the entertainment world. Most of us exercise it frequently. When we exert ourselves to use our friends, family, colleagues, and contacts to get our child into a particular playgroup, school, college, university, training scheme, job, or social milieu, we are using dynastic power. Dynastic power is about pulling strings for your child's social advancement. It is about connections, relationships, and influence. Above all it concerns access. When you invite your most influential contact to make a speech at your daughter's wedding, you are calling upon dynastic power. It can often be observed in the choice of godparents. Dynastic power is employed everywhere from the shopfloor to the boardroom – at all social levels and in all countries. It is a parental power much in use.

Dynastic power can cause social damage. But as it is universally exercised, it is also universally monitored. When it gets out of hand, sooner or later society puts the brakes on. In the fifteenth and sixteenth centuries the Papacy's outrageous misuse of nepotism (the Pope's natural sons were politely known as 'nephews') was partly responsible for the huge revision culminating in the Counter-Reformation. By the middle of the last century, the British Civil Service had become a hotbed of dynastic preferment. Gladstone finally put a stop to it in 1870 when he approved the principle of competitive entrance at the top end of the service. In industry and in business, inept use of dynastic power is plainly self-defeating. Dynastic power can only create opportunity. It does not guarantee achievement.

Of course all parents want the best for our children – and

dynastic power is often the way we provide opportunities for them. It is a very powerful tool in our parental kit, and it can create long-lasting repercussions. For these reasons we need to be very careful when we use it, and particularly careful in checking our motives.

Dangers in misuse

When we make mistakes in our use of dynastic power, it is usually someone else who pays. The one who pays most heavily is the son or daughter whom we are supposedly trying to help. We've all known people who have been forced into unsuitable careers by dynastic-minded parents. We've probably all known mothers like Penny.

Penny's only son was the apple of her eye. Davey was a clever, articulate little boy but his determination not to apply himself to his schoolwork defied all her efforts. How much work he was willing to do depended, it seemed, entirely on whether he happened to get on with his teacher. It was unfortunate for Davey that the last teacher he had in his primary school did not take kindly to him. This was in the time of the problematic eleven-plus examination – and Davey did not pass it. He could not follow his sister to the local grammar school. Davey was mortified and very disappointed.

Propelled by dynastic power, Penny decided to do all she could to get Davey into the grammar school. Nobody disputed that Davey was clever. She began pulling out the stops. She found out the name of the most respected child psychologist in her city and arranged for an appointment for Davey to have a full IQ and personality test. Davey and the eminent doctor got on famously – and after extensive testing, she pronounced him exceptionally bright, with an IQ in the top 3 per cent of the community. Penny was pleased but not surprised. She was aware – as were all his teachers – that Davey was clever. However, *they* said he was lazy. Penny believed he was understimulated. Armed with the expert's opinion she launched herself on the local education authority. It did not take her long to get their conditional approval for Davey to go to the grammar school – conditional upon his acceptance by the headmaster.

The headmaster was tougher than the bureaucrats. He was used to dealing with parents like Penny. He insisted that Davey do another test. In this test Davey did not do well. It was formal and depended more on factual accuracy, good spelling, and numeracy, rather than comprehension and problem-solving – in which he shone. The headmaster did not think the child was right for grammar school. He did not want to take Davey and said so.

But Penny was determined. She used every argument in the book – and a few that weren't. She referred to Davey's IQ, his expectations, his potential. She cited the example of his sister, a hardworking, industrious little girl two years older than Davey. She implied that the local authority had given approval for Davey's admission. She talked in veiled terms of the damage that adverse publicity could do, if a child with Davey's quantified intelligence was refused the chance of an academic education. As you will have guessed, she got him in.

Davey did not do well at the grammar school. Whether the Head had accurately foreseen that Davey did not yet have the discipline to undertake the kind of formal, old-fashioned study expected by the school, or whether the Head's misgivings had filtered down to the staff, it was hard for Penny to establish. But Davey's results slithered from bad to worse. He became so disaffected that even extra tutors (provided by Penny) made no dent in the armour of studied indifference which Davey had by now built up. In his fourth year he was truanting regularly – and was finally expelled at the age of 16. It is impossible to say whether the outcome would have been different if he had gone to the creamed-off comprehensive in the district. The result might easily have been the same. On the other hand, Davey certainly did not flourish in the grammar school.

Penny could have done something quite different. She could have left the matter alone and let Davey learn the invaluable lesson that refusal to work brings no benefits. At the grammar school Davey suffered from being behind in his work but he also suffered because he knew perfectly well (how could he not?) that he had not *earned* the right to be where he was. In the long run, Penny did her son no favours. Determined to get the best for her clever little boy, Penny had hurled herself into a battle, which she won. Unfortunately, it led to Davey losing out all round.

Checking our own motives

The sad thing about this story is that Penny acted as well as she could – *at that time*. She did not know enough about herself to recognize that it wasn't altogether for Davey's sake that she was moving heaven and earth. It was quite as much for her own sake. She had not been honest about her motives. She did not think (or know) enough to check this out beforehand. In fact she only came to grips with it after Davey had been summarily expelled. When this happened, she was forced to look at her own parenting and the part she had played in getting him into the school in the first place. Through her pain she found enough honesty to admit that her motives had been far from pure.

Penny wanted her son to go to the grammar school for a number of reasons, not least its academic reputation. She reckoned it provided a more reliable route to the professional career she envisaged for Davey. She also thought that he needed the supposedly superior teaching available at the grammar school because of his superior intelligence. But there is a catch here, which Penny refused to consider. Intelligence, if not exercised, is not a lot of use.

Exams may appear to be a bore and even irrelevant – but discovering how to pass them can itself be seen as a test of intelligence. For all his brightness, Davey clearly had not understood this simple fact, and was easily overtaken by all the supposed tortoises who had actually applied themselves to their work. Penny did not take this into account. Moreover, in planning to replace Davey's disappointment with undeserved success, she was not taking care of his best interests. Why should he bother to work anywhere or anytime if results could so easily be manipulated by a bit of swift footwork on the part of the family?

That was not all. When she had come to terms with all this, it finally emerged that she also would have been ashamed that *her son* would be seen by friends and neighbours to have failed – in her terms. He would not be wearing the distinctive uniform of the grammar school. This was very embarrassing for her to acknowledge – even to herself (it seemed so trivial) – but when she had *admitted* her own pusillanimous motives, she actually began to feel better about herself. She accepted that she had acted unwisely and mistakenly, but recognized that she had learned an invaluable lesson – that she could not control her son's life or actions. She must look to herself and her own behaviour and leave her son to work out his own destiny.

When it comes to deciding whether or not to put your dynastic power into use, it is vital to check your own personal involvement.

The fact that you *can* open a door for your child does not mean you have to.

Is your son really up to the job – or are you kidding yourself, because maybe *you* would have given your eye-teeth for such a chance at his age? Is he going to use the opportunity well, or does he need more time where he is?

Are you quite certain of your motives for *not* supporting your daughter for that job she wants so badly? Could it be that she might outshine you? Has she had advantages you didn't have yourself? Do you secretly want her to struggle the way you did – though her circumstances (thanks to you) are very different from your own? Do you really want her to succeed, or would it take the gloss off your own success? What are your *real* reasons for not helping her?

A classic case of misuse

I once came across a father of two sons. He was divorced, and his boys lived with their mother. This man (whom we will call Bernard) had achieved considerable eminence in his field. He favoured his elder son Max, not least because the youth was always agreeable and seldom bothered to argue with him. When Max was 17, Bernard announced proudly that he had arranged an interview for the boy with a good chance of a job in the industry. He didn't need to say (but he said it all the same) that the business was almost impossible to break into without contacts.

For reasons that never were fully explained, Max didn't get to the interview. He *said* he had gone to the wrong place. We might speculate that the youth did not want to work in the business but had got the measure of his father and simply decided that actions speak louder than words.

Sam, the younger boy, was very different from Max. He was not at all diplomatic with his father. He was involved and enthusiastic, impatient of pomposity, and quite capable of contradicting and arguing with his father. But Sam loved and needed his father deeply, was desperate to win his approval, and longed to be as favoured as his brother.

Now Sam at 14 was a splendid tennis player. He began winning tournaments – pretty much on his own unaided efforts since the tennis coach at his school was a joke. When he was going to play in a very big tournament he asked his father for a really good racquet. His level of play did require first-class equipment, and his father (unlike his mother) could afford it. To Sam's dismay, the racquet his father gave him was cheap and inferior. Mercifully, a friend came to the rescue. Sam played really well. So well that he was 'discovered'. He was approached and offered coaching at a top level. The catch for Sam was the cost. With the best will in the world, the general expenses were going to cost a great deal more than his mother could afford. He approached his father. And his father said no.

Bernard's behaviour to his two sons is almost a classic example of how a parent can misuse his dynastic power. Bernard obviously never fully consulted Max about going into his business. Max clearly neither wanted nor intended to work with his father. In fact he became a P.E. teacher. Sam on the other hand wanted very much to become a professional tennis player – and had already proved his ability. Bernard's refusal to help him take advantage of an excellent training opportunity can most likely be traced to unacknowledged jealousy of his athletic younger son. Jealousy is a not uncommon feeling in parents. It's unworthy, but it's human. We can't help having the feeling – most of us get a twinge of it now and then – but we can help what we do about it. Regrettably, Bernard acted it out.

Dynastic power can give parents unrivalled opportunities to try to live in the future – through our offspring. We can open doors for them, as Bernard did for Max, or we can refuse, as he did with Sam. Whether our children use any opportunities we offer them is not up to us. We cannot control anyone's future – not even our own. We can only control our own actions.

In the end the proper use of dynastic power boils down to this: what will most help your children to fulfil their whole potential? Only when we have cleared ourselves completely out of the equation, can we answer that question with proper clarity and arrive at a decision that is right for ourselves and for the child. We then use our dynastic power most effectively.

But providing contacts and influencing people is not all there is to dynastic power.

Parent-child apartheid

Dynastic power is also about handing on our skills and knowledge and wisdom to our children – and it is a very different matter today from time past.

We live in a society which is distinguished by parent-child apartheid. This is a new thing, for the very interesting reason that children as such, are a relatively new invention. Until the late Middle Ages, young people were just that – young people. When they outgrew infancy, children were regarded simply as smaller people from whom expectations of work and understanding were graduated according to size. (You can read more about this in *Centuries of Childhood*, Philippe Ariès, Penguin 1973.)

Compulsory education changed all that. Schools for the upper classes had existed in Britain since the mid-16th century but in 1880 compulsory education was introduced for the whole country – and the schoolchild emerged. And with the school-child, the beginnings of a special kind of separation between adults and children. As Ariès put it, 'Henceforth it was recognized that the child was not ready for life and that he had to be subjected to a special treatment, a sort of quarantine, before he was allowed to join the adults.'

That apartheid has grown. Children are not welcome in the workplace and parents are not allowed in the schoolroom. The iconoclastic educator Ivan Illich compares schools to temples which no one may enter other than the high priests and a privileged elite. The elite are people aged between 5 and 18. Teachers of course are the priests.

Likewise children may not penetrate the sacred realms of adult work. Children no longer learn about work from their parents, except for unpaid work which is carried on at home – such as housework and DIY. There are a few small pockets in which children can experience work with their parents, in small shops, farms, cafes, and vicarages, and among artists and craftspeople. In the main, children are taboo in the workplace.

Consequently, a huge area of child-parent involvement has disappeared. Parents no longer teach their children the skills and secrets of the job. Children do not learn from their parents about the world of work – the slog and the tension, the discipline and the excitement, the politics, the pressure and the pleasure.

Left-behind parents?

For a time, after schooling became universal and compulsory, parents could still pass on some educational skills to their children. But nowadays it is hard to find a parent who can enter into the companionable task of helping with homework or prep. This is not because parents do not want to, but because they feel inadequate. A Gallup poll in 1987 of 600 parents throughout the country indicated that about half wanted to help but 70 per cent said they lacked the knowledge or ability and a further 19 per cent said they were too out of date. Teaching methods change every decade, brand new subjects appear, and of course there's the new technology. Apparently the gulf is growing wider.

According to Professor Tom Stonier of Bradford University, we are subject to four distinct time-clocks. There's a biological clock which takes thousands of years to rotate full circle and modify our biology. Then there's a cultural clock, which revolves according to changes in family, work, and institutions and which needs one or two generations to complete its cycle. The technological clock revolves in one to two decades. And now we have yet another clock to take account of. It's the information technology clock – and it whizzes round in just three to five years. Try keeping up with that!

What knowledge and wisdom and skills can we now hand on and how do we go about it? Our lives are already jammed with things we must see and see to – things that didn't even exist a hundred years ago: holidays abroad, road tax, house insurance, parking fines, the Dow Jones Index, soaps, telephone bills, mortgage rate changes, to name but a few. So on account of *our* work and *their* school, on account of the calls and myriad demands of our modern world, we have limited time and space to know our children – and *to make ourselves known to them.*

How our children see us

Fathers are often very different at home from at work. We all know the man who is reliable, responsible, and well-regarded in his job, but who unwinds at home so completely that he is, quite literally, a different person. This father's splendid professional qualities are seldom, if ever, disclosed to his children. They do not experience their father at his best, but at his least admirable, slobbing drearily in front of the television or returning the worse for wear from the pub.

At one level children learn about us all the time, because the human child is born to imitate. It is constantly watching, absorbing and remembering. If you want to teach a child to throw a ball, you do it. You don't talk about it and give directions. You throw the ball a couple of times and the child will copy. Watch your children playing 'mummies and daddies'. You may well find yourself drawn to the life – gestures, turns of speech, behaviour – all meticulously mimicked. But *you* know and *I* know that there's more to you than that.

Without superior knowledge and work skills to offer, you could say that we parents are now pared down to the bone. What is left?

What is left to offer?

The skill of skills

What is left, quite simply, is ourselves. In the end it's the only thing we do have to give. But to do this, most of us need to get to work on our ability to communicate. We are not, most of us, particularly good at communicating. We share our thoughts, but not our feelings. But it is our feelings which propel us into action. Buttoned up ourselves, we expect others to know how we feel by telepathy – and become resentful or hurt if they get it wrong. We make assumptions about how others feel, failing to realize that their history is not our history and that, unless they tell us, we may never know.

Yet parents are the original communicators. When you take your new baby in your arms, your baby learns its first lesson in trust. In your voice is the knowledge of comfort. In your eyes is affirmation of its very existence. Compared with our children's ability to pick up computer-speak we may feel inadequate. But in the matter of communication – the skill that underpins all other skills – they are verily babes in the wood without our help and guidance. On to us falls fair and square the task of teaching them how properly to communicate.

Listening

Communication, the kind I'm talking about here, is not about information, nor is it about being articulate. Communication starts at the other end. It starts, not with talking, but with listening.

Listening is an art which remarkably few people develop. Oddly enough most parents begin well. They will wake with a start when a new baby so much as whimpers in its sleep. A couple of years later this faculty seems to disappear without trace.

Listening (in the present context) has little to do with your hearing. One of my dearest friends has a hearing disability but he's one of the most gifted listeners I know. Listening is an activity which involves the whole self – physical, mental, and emotional.

In an up-dated job description for parents, listening (and thereby teaching your child to listen) ranks high. When you listen, really listen, you give your whole self. You are open. Good listeners even sit in an open way: relaxed, arms loose. You physically open yourself up to your child. You still yourself, become still inside. You put aside all thought of things to say. You are just a receiver. You are totally aware of your child, of the whole person of your child.

When you are really listening, you have suspended judgement. You are not poised there, ready to interject, to get across your own message. For now, you have no message, nothing to say. You want nothing. You are not looking for facts, for excuses, for reasons. For this moment only, you have all the time there is. You are a receiver and you are allowing your child to be truly heard, to be totally accepted.

Very often something strange happens. You hear not only what is said, but what is *not* said. Something clicks inside and you understand the words that are left out – and sometimes even why they have been left out. It is a process that is awesome and moving and brings you very close to your child. It is difficult to describe. It is understanding and being understood in practice.

When you listen in this way, you automatically teach your child to do the same – and it has spin-offs in every direction. The great thing is that you can start any time. There's no closing date.

The different levels of communication

We live and connect with each other on different levels. There's the fingertip level: 'It's going to rain, better take an umbrella'. 'Did you put the cat out?' 'I've got a late meeting, I won't be back till nine.' This is also the level at which we gossip: 'Do you know what Deirdre told me today . . .?'

The second level involves the head. It's an information level. Here we discuss facts – anything from the price of jeans to the structure of DNA. And ideas: 'With a bit of ingenuity, we could put a cupboard over the door' 'What about turning the diagram upside down?' My child may be better informed about some subjects than me – I can listen. I can even practise listening when he or she is telling me stuff I knew before he or she was born. If I am weary from a hard day at work it may take an act of will to stop my eyes glazing over and a quelling put-down issuing from my lips. To do this I may have to remember my manners. My child needs to know the best of me. I might even learn something.

At the first two levels I have not involved much of myself at all. The subjects are factual and neutral. But at the third level of discourse, the real person I am begins to emerge: this is the level of belief. When I speak whereof I believe, I begin to emerge as a person. From what I believe my children learn a great deal about who I am, because they will find out where my heart is.

And now we get to gut level, the level of feeling. It's sad to relate but many people never learn how to communicate at this level, other than at peak moments of passion – pleasurable or painful. But in truth this is where we live most of the time. Our feelings inform our thoughts, our judgements, and our actions. When we report them we gain some control over them.

Warts and all

Listening, as we saw, is half the process. The other half is having the courage to tell them something about the person you really are – warts and all.

If you think your child needs to tell you something but is either too frightened or ashamed to say, you can help. This does *not* mean sitting them down with the stern demand to tell you the truth. You will need some quiet space and time to be with them – whether they are 8 or 18 or 28. Then you can tell them about a time when *you* yourself were frightened or humiliated. What *is* important is that you tell the truth, tell what really happened and how you felt at the time. If you disclose something very private and difficult, however silly and trivial it might be, this will be clear to the other person. Unless you have consistently given your child the example of confidence betrayed, you need not fear that the child will be untrustworthy. In the main, adults much more often betray trust than children do.

It is high time parents got out of the way of being always in the right. How often do you admit you were in the wrong? Oh, not about something concrete like being late for a train. I'm talking about admitting to being unkind out of envy, to being irritable because of intolerance or impatience, admitting to being depressed because you've been disappointed about something. Surprisingly we don't lose face by an admission of frailty. We gain humanity.

Children learn mostly by observation and example. Having problems with emotions is part of the human condition. Our workload as parents includes helping them to identify, acknowledge and handle their feelings – even if, like a new teacher, we sometimes have to learn with them as we go along, barely keeping one page ahead of the class!

Denying the 'not-good' feelings

As we live through our day, we get feelings all the time. Most of us are willing only to recognize the 'good' feelings, affection, friendliness, gratitude, approval, liking, loving. It's the 'not-good' feelings we neglect and repress, as we saw earlier – feelings like irritation, disappointment, envy, anger, fear and suspicion. At times I have felt all of these feelings in varying degrees in relation to my sons – and I am very sure other parents do too.

But when we repress our negative feelings about our nearest and dearest (specifically our children) we are surely set for a blowout. Theirs *or* ours. The blowout may be a sudden unexpected fury on our part. It may smoulder darkly in a child and lead to a permanent rift when that child is grown up.

I did not know at all how to express my 'bad' feelings, since in my own parents' home (as in so many others) it was unthinkable to acknowledge that you felt anything but happy. In practice, this meant I was known to have a filthy temper at times, while one of my sisters was labelled sulky. My father on occasion raged and bellowed through the house and finally shut himself in his room, refusing to have anything to do with anyone. My mother for her part would go red in the face and spout bitter recriminations. Nobody ever cried – unless in bad physical pain. No connection was made between any of these occurrences and our feelings. If the question was ever asked, 'How are you feeling?' it was correctly assumed that the questioner was enquiring after one's bodily health. The proper response was of the order: 'My cold's gone now, thank you'.

Neither my mother nor my father knew how to handle the shadow side of themselves, so I entered the outside world without the faintest idea that I had often been very fearful, very angry, and very isolated. I thought I was honest, because I was exceedingly law abiding and owned up if I had actually *done* something wrong. I was not aware that I was quite dishonest about my feelings – even with the people closest to me. I did not know how to admit to disappointment, irritation, shame, envy and jealousy. I would smile, put on a front – and then *act* irritable or moody or depressed. It was all about pride and courage. You didn't let your side down. Pride and courage were both needed to keep the smile pasted on your face, so you never had to let on that you were disappointed (or hurt or miserable or whatever).

About 15 years ago I came to a very rocky patch. Many things were wrong in my life, and the smile I still wore could now be best described as a nervous rictus. I was forced to reappraise my life if I was to keep it – and began to discover that it was both possible and safe to get in touch with my feelings, to acknowledge and trust them. It was even possible (with a great intake of breath) to share them. That often did take courage, but instead of pride, I found it necessary to learn the healing power of humility.

In the years since then I have also discovered that my interior dishonesty was not unique to my family. It is commonplace. Most people seem to have been born into families where it was not done to have 'bad' feelings. Most parents of today's parents denied their negative emotions – and taught their children, in turn, to deny them.

We do not have to perpetuate the errors of our parents. We *can* do things differently. Our parents' mistakes were buttressed by society, as we have seen. In the main they got away with it. We do not have that option. Parents today are stripped naked, without social support. We really have to communicate with our children. We don't have anything else.

Fairytale work

There aren't many people who don't like the sound of their own voice. Happily one aspect of parenthood caters for this quite beautifully. Dynastic power specifically indicates that we do the talking.

From the beginning of time children have listened to their

mothers and fathers telling stories about ... well, the beginning of time. How the world was created, how seas and mountains, meadows and animals, fish and birds and humans first appeared. They have learnt myths of gods and devils, fairies and angels, ghosties and ghoulies, goodies and baddies, cowboys and Indians, cops and robbers ... tribal myths and local myths and global myths. Here in the west our children have a vast heritage. They are heir to the stories of Greece and Rome and Israel. They inherit the Brothers Grimm and Hans Christian Andersen and William Shakespeare – everything from Cinderella to Mahatma Ghandi. (Mythic people and events are not always in the distant past.)

But beyond and above all this, children have a right to knowledge of their roots, their own family stories. And you hold the key to unlock that magic door. There's an endless fascination, especially for very young children, in hearing about when you were young yourself, and about your parents and their parents. As soon as someone becomes a grandparent, they seem to grasp this fact – but it is not solely a grandparent's prerogative. It is also a parent's. This is a part of the job which is more perk than work. It's hardly a chore to talk about yourself. Even the grotty bits enchant the young. They agonize with your sorrows and delight in the awful things you got away with. They laugh at your worst jokes. They are a marvellous audience – better than a saloon bar any day.

A good memory bank

Singing and making music together is traditional and for very good reasons. It releases deep and ancient resonances, and builds a happy memory bank for the future. We remember occasions when we have sung together: singing songs round fires, in buses, in charabancs, in school choirs, and at parties where someone has brought a guitar or played the piano – pop songs and folk songs and sacred songs and rude songs. Singing is therapeutic because it is one of the rare activities which engages simultaneously the left and right sides of our frontal lobes. Even quite simple songs engage us fully and satisfy a primitive need for balance. Singing together is a basic right for both parents and children – it is a golden thread which binds families in every society that inhabits our planet. Don't underrate it.

It even has practical uses. When 'I Spy' ran out of steam on long drives, singing with my three young sons would guarantee many peaceful miles. Lots of people are convinced they can't sing – in fact almost everyone can, and the nice thing about singing with the family is that it absolutely doesn't matter if you don't sing well. If mother or father sounds like an afflicted donkey, that's fine too. Your humble but valiant efforts will become part of the family story – and the donkey always could turn out to be a wizard on a comb or the spoons.

The heritage of games

Humans are game players. Regrettably many families play their games by proxy these days – via television. But playing games with your children is a definite part of the job and not necessarily confined to Christmas.

Games come in all sizes and guises. Playing a game is like putting a punctuation mark in the prose of everyday life. A game sets a different scene. Preparations must be made, rules have to be agreed, and ordinary considerations are for the time suspended. These actions take place whether the game is as simple as noughts and crosses (a pencil and paper) or as elaborate as tennis (getting a court, racquets, decent balls, suitable clothes).

If you really can't get out with a bat and ball there are games to suit all tastes. There must be a thousand card games, board games, word games, number games, and computer games. Some parents find it difficult to play a game with a young child because they just have to win. Or, worse, they lose so condescendingly that the child wins the game but loses heart. There are ways out. Play games which depend not on skill or intelligence or knowledge, but on the fall of the dice or the turn of a card. Have a go at 'Snap' rather than rummy, Snakes and Ladders rather than Mastermind or Trivial Pursuit. There's Junior Scrabble – which doesn't permit such complex verbal skills as the adult version, or stick with draughts – it is less demanding than chess. 'Murder' is easier than 'charades'.

Dynastic power requires that we do not overlook the old games in the novelty of electronics. It is the wholly personal interaction in our games which is valuable. When we play games together, we learn a great deal about each other. We can use the opportunity to let our children discover our values and our standards. Are we fair? Honest? Fun? Without even noticing it, we are learning and teaching and making our children's acquaintance on a different level from everyday living. We are also making history, family history.

A very successful man had three children. He loved them very much in his own fashion. He gave them splendid toys and presents, the gifts getting bigger and better as his career progressed and they grew older. But the eldest said, 'My father would have laid down his life for me, but he wouldn't give me half an hour of his time.' The second one said, 'I cannot think of a single thing my father ever taught me.' The third one said sadly, 'When I look at other fathers I sometimes don't think I ever really had one. His career was his child.'

I do not think many fathers would like to be remembered that way.

Gender roles

Dynastic power involves gender. At a very deep level we always measure all women by our own mother and all men by our own father. So too will our children. It's an awesome responsibility when you think about it.

In the past it was traditional to divide up duties and charac- teristics according to gender, and try to ensure that boys were encouraged to demonstrate the qualities that were said to be 'manly' and girls to express those which were supposedly 'feminine'.

Being manly meant being physically courageous, self-assured, purposeful, job-oriented, ambitious, interested in the world, in ideas and in public activity – and in games. Initiative and indi- viduality were definitely manly. A good man was protective of his woman and children.

Being feminine meant being physically attractive, modest, pliable, deferential, interested in domestic pursuits, clothes, children, the family and the Church. Initiative and individuality were strongly discouraged in females. A good woman was responsive to her man's needs, wishes and demands.

The world was a boy's oyster. Within reason, he could choose his life's work, secure in the knowledge that his meals, his children and his domestic needs would always be looked after by somebody else throughout his life. His mother, wife or sister would make sure he always had his meals prepared, clean clothes and a comfortable bed. He could give his whole attention to his work and his leisure. In return he would be expected to provide economic support for the women of his household. In practice almost every father would expect at least one son to follow in his footsteps, whatever his business, trade or profession. Dynastic power started early.

Girls did not have choice. Their gender, not their inclinations or gifts, determined their future. They were taught to serve, by way of domestic pursuits. They served in turn their fathers, brothers, husbands, children, elderly relatives and needy members of the local community. They were invariably taught cooking, cleaning, mending, household and child management. If they did not have a male to support them, they practised these skills in other households – as maids, nannies, cooks, chambermaids, nurses, governesses or teachers.

Of course this is not the whole story. Throughout history vast numbers of women have supported their families through every kind of work – from estate management to mining. Medieval illuminated manuscripts show wonderful pictures of women actively pursuing any job you can think of. But the brutish market forces of the industrial revolution peeled back some very dark pictures. In the Trades Union Council archives we read, 'Mr. E., a manufacturer, informed us that he employed married females exclusively on the power looms, especially those who have families at home dependent on them for support; they are attentive, doubly more so than unmarried women and are compelled to use their utmost exertions to procure the necessities of life.'

Gender-conditioning of women has always taken place, not least because of the old truism, 'gender is destiny'. Until women had the possibility of real control over their child-bearing, which did not take place till about 20 years ago, they were inevitably subject to their gender, and all that it implies.

Gender is no longer destiny

Today's parents need to think about this. Our sons today are not growing up in a world where women are inevitably prepared to take care of a man's entire emotional life – or even his dirty clothes. A wise mother whose four sons are required to take responsibility for all the washing up in her house said to me proudly, 'I mean to be friends with my future daughters-in-law!'

And daughters need to know that even if mummy never did any 'real' work, they themselves had better aim for a proper career with future prospects. Marriage is not a secure job these days. One in three marriages fail. In most broken marriages, women have to take on the childcare. They almost always get inadequate financial support. A cynical single parent recently said to her daughter, 'I'll be quite happy to come to your tenth marriage, but I want to see you qualified before the first.' Parents with daughters who are reluctant to get qualifications might suggest a holiday job with a single parent organization.

From a purely functional point of view it is clearly our duty as parents to consider carefully the conditioning we give to our sons and daughters. It is written in the job description that we do our best to prepare them for the real world.

Conditioning our children

We condition our children both by being role-models for them, and also by what we expect of them. If we go on expecting our daughters to be decorative and pliable and empty-headed, they'll be inadequately prepared for the future. If we let our sons get away with domestic irresponsibility (in every sense), we effectively infantilize them. It is, after all, common sense to make sure that every able-bodied person contributes to the housework. Not just the nice jobs, like cooking, but the less appealing jobs like cleaning the lavatory. It is reasonable to expect that everyone should know how to take care of their own bodily needs – cooking, cleaning, washing up, bed-making, tidying up, ironing and mending – and be able to care for someone else should the occasion arise.

These are goals we can properly expect to aim for. But providing an up-to-date role-model for our children is quite another thing.

Marjorie and Alan had a splendid, even-handed relationship, and two young sons. Marjorie did her work from home, and Alan had good flexible hours as a specialist journalist. He spent a great deal of time with the boys, playing with them, taking them away for weekends, and teaching them all manner of things. This freed Marjorie for her own work and interests. It was a very happy family. But Alan hated housework and especially he hated cooking. He could hardly even bring himself to heat a can of baked beans (unless it was over a camp fire!). Marjorie, mock-serious, said one day, 'Sometimes I wonder whether despite all the rest, the picture my sons will have is of me standing in front of the cooker!'

In the circumstances, Marjorie's concern was a bit over the top. Alan was a great role-model of child caring. But it is worth thinking about how our children may perceive us. It is our example as people, not the words that we speak, which has the greatest effect. If you are not entirely happy with the role-model you are providing for your children, you can begin to change it, little bit by little bit. People who say, 'That's how I am. I'm like that and I'll always be like that' do not speak truth.

We all change all the time. Our whole body changes second by second. The events which happen to us, the people we encounter, modify and temper how we feel and think and act. Change is inevitable. What's more, we can decide *how* we change. It is never too late.

COERCIVE POWER

'Our job as parents is to give our children not just shelter and protection, food and sustenance, but a sense of order ... they need to know that their parents love them enough to give them sensible rules and boundaries ...'

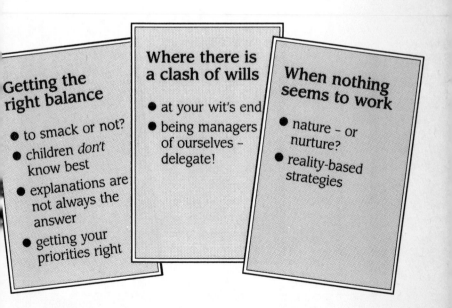

Getting the right balance

- to smack or not?
- children *don't* know best
- explanations are not always the answer
- getting your priorities right

Where there is a clash of wills

- at your wit's end
- being managers of ourselves – delegate!

When nothing seems to work

- nature – or nurture?
- reality-based strategies

Getting the right balance

This power is about force – and we all use it from the very start of our baby's life. Every time you pull your little one away from danger, when you drag a toddler off a busy road, when you haul a child back from a precarious balcony, you are using coercive power. Like all our powers, coercive power, of itself, is neutral. It can be used for good or for ill. Child sexual abuse and battering are the sinister aspects of a power which is vital for the safety of the new small members of our race.

Coercion can be verbal as well as physical. When you insist that an unwilling child finishes its homework or supper, you are coercing the child. Coercion means compelling somebody by means of authority or superior force to do something against their will. Words can be just as effective – or just as damaging – as physical abuse.

Coercive force is an essential tool. Parents have to coerce children – in one way or other – to do things they sometimes don't want to do. The purpose of coercive force is control. It is, however a power of diminishing returns.

To smack or not to smack?

Physical coercion includes pulling, pushing, lifting, shaking, or holding a child. It can also mean smacking it. Few parents have not done most of these things, in moments of peril or anger – or immediately afterwards. All parents must have wanted to.

Smacking? Most expectant and very new parents cannot bear

the thought of it – and believe they never will do it. The majority of parents (with the possible exception of those who have a single child) find they resort to it now and then. The rationale includes the following: a small slap may save a thousand words; it releases some of the parent's own steam; an instant physical slap administered in the heat of the moment can be more effective and less frightening than a punishment waiting to be delivered.

Other parents consider that all smacking is completely wrong. In their view it is unacceptable bullying. A small and defenceless child is seen to be totally at the mercy of a large and menacing adult. From this viewpoint smacking is a sign of moral bankruptcy, of parental defeat.

Here is another area where parents have no cut-and-dried guidelines. You will, of course, decide for yourself. Up till now parents have been completely free to decide – but there are moves to make the smacking of children illegal in the home as it is now illegal in schools.

Sometimes a child may seem to drive us mad. On a few occasions I have felt so frayed that I thought I would do my child a damage. But there *is* a cut-out point for most of us, and there was for me. I stopped in time. But I can understand the nightmare of a faulty cut-out. Nonetheless I do know this: *if ever I had hurt a child I would seek help immediately.* It would take an enormous amount of courage – but the alternative is too dreadful to contemplate.

Physical coercion is a power of diminishing returns. As the child grows, words and deeds become infinitely more effective. A baby *must* be pulled away from fire: a six year old can be yelled at.

Children need control, even if they don't exactly appear to welcome it. It provides them with a sense of safety. Somebody cares enough to bother about them – even when they are naughty. Especially when they're naughty. A child who makes its own rules feels – *and is* – unloved and insecure.

Children *don't* know best

I wrote earlier about parents who have difficulty in controlling their children – in making rules, setting boundaries and making them stick. A lot of this is a hangover from Spock and the sixties culture. At that time, many people interpreted the message of Dr Spock to mean that children know best about everything. If children were allowed to follow their instincts, it was argued, they would grow up free and emotionally healthy. It was a sort of 20th-century version of Rousseau's 'noble savage' – nature in the raw was perfect. This carried over into education, where the theory was worked out that children would learn best if they were never coerced, but allowed to work only when they wanted to. This overlooked the undeniable fact that few children would voluntarily choose to sit down to long division or grammar when the alternative was 'Dr Who' on the box. In consequence vast numbers of understimulated, semi-literate, or bored children roamed the world. (As a matter of fact, bored children were a new phenomenon at this time. Until then children had never been bored – or at least did not say so. Children have been moaning, 'I'm bored' ever since – and very boring it is for everyone else.)

It is remarkable that educationalists could ever have expected children *naturally* to want to read and write. Our human ancestors go back 50 million years and writing was invented only about 4 thousand years ago. Not long in the overall scheme of things, you will agree. Until the present century, only a puny number of priests and scholars here and there have ever been privy to the mystery of the written word. The rest of humanity has managed quite well all those 50 million years without any apparent need or urge to read and write. In Britain – ahead of most countries – universal literacy only became available a mere hundred years ago. If children *want* to read and write it's because of imitation or personal quirk. Natural it isn't.

However, by the end of the seventies it became evident that absolute freedom was corrupting absolutely – and in education, a quiet reversal of policy took place. Today children no longer drift through open-plan classrooms wandering from project to project as the whim takes them. They are no longer assumed to know entirely what is best for them.

But at home the myth still seems to persist that in some mysterious way children know best and should not be thwarted. Parents don't actually say it: they act it. Let's clear the confusion. In a very *limited* sense, babies and small children do know best. In the simple physical functions – eating and sleeping and defecating, babies are self-regulating, like the very best watches. Their internal messages are valid – provided the child is loved and healthy. A parent needs only to decode the information to be able to come up with a content and well-adjusted infant.

But, in matters of personal safety, and in social matters –

anything that involves other people – children need direction. They do *not* come into the world fully equipped for all the situations and social interactions they will meet, and they need guidance. They do not instinctively understand possession and property. They are not born knowing the rules of the road. They have no prior knowledge of manners. They do not intuitively grasp the requirements of the specific society into which they are born. They have to be taught these things.

Mercifully, children absorb most of their learning by imitation. Which fact takes us right into the centre of our task.

To an enormous extent our children's socialization is determined by our own behaviour. Our job as parents therefore requires that we do our best always to act as we wish our children to act.

Respect and courtesy are not idle words. They mean small concrete things – like not prying into your child's secret drawer, or not embarrassing your child by picking on him or her in public. It means keeping our act clean. Children are expert observers and mimics. We can save ourselves a lot of pain by capitalizing on this fact, giving them not the worst, but the best of ourselves to observe and imitate.

However, with the best examples in the world, it must be said that some of society's requirements are neither particularly reasonable nor self-evident, and many conflict with powerful primary instincts. For this reason coercive power is a very useful and important tool.

Help for the endangered parent

I would like to make clear that this book is written for the large numbers of loving and well-intentioned parents who are often unconfident and uneasy about the job. It does not address the problems of parents at the extremes. Parents who physically or sexually assault their children are at an extreme. They (and their partners) need proper help – *now*. Without action, without help, the situation will only get worse, never better. A telephone call to the Samaritans or to Parents Anonymous could be a start. Parents Anonymous is a self-help organization for parents who understand – who have harmed their children or feel they might be in danger of doing so. At the other extreme are parents who simply don't *want* to try to control their children. Parents who have given up. They also need help, but it is likely their children are already receiving professional attention of one kind or another.

This book, however, is for people in the middle – which means most of us. People who don't (most of the time) need experts: but who sometimes get to the end of their tether. Parents who dearly love their children and want the best for them: but are not always sure what *is* the best for them. Parents who enjoy their children most of the time but who once in a while would like to send them smartly back where they came from. This usually happens when all the other options have run out – blandishments, rewards, encouragement, and explanations. Above all, explanations.

Explanations are not always the answer

There is a mystique about explanations. Many modern parents have read books about bringing up children, in which the idea is promoted that if you explain to your children all the reasons you want them to do something, they will instantly down cudgels and do it. Nice going if it works. The trouble is, children are no different from *people*. And people on the whole cannot necessarily be talked into doing things they actively do not wish to do. Try getting your partner to spend an evening with the detested Aunt Carrie. Explain it all: Carrie is ill . . . it would be a kindness . . . she has so few visitors . . . it's only one evening out of a lifetime . . . it would make *you* happy. And so on. You might get action, but then again you might not. Children are no different.

Getting your priorities right

It is good management to avoid having to use coercive power whenever possible. The line of least resistance may be good sense. Beyond babyhood and very early childhood, coercive power is the power of last resort.

To avert confrontation, *get your priorities in order.* A lot of conflict happens because we haven't thought things through very carefully. Let's suppose you want your child to come on that family visit to the tiresome Aunt Carrie. Understandably the child doesn't want to accompany you. You will have your own reasons for suggesting the child go with you – but if these reasons include, say, wanting company for yourself to take the boredom out of the visit, or wanting to show your child off to other relatives who will be there (two unworthy but not uncommon reasons), then think again. If *you* have decided, for yourself, to make the pilgrimage, fine. But why inflict it on the hapless child? Do you *need* a head-on collision?

However – please don't take this example too literally. I'm not advocating that children should always be allowed to determine when and where they will deign to grace family occasions. Like parents, children have family duties – and visiting the old, the infirm, and the unloved is certainly one of them. The point at issue to consider is *your* motivation.

Our job as parents is to give our children not just shelter and protection, food and sustenance, but a sense of order. They need to know that there are parents who love them enough to give them sensible rules and boundaries. The operative word is sensible.

When there is a clash of wills

No question, there are times when we have to force our children to do things against their will. If they had any sense and knew what was good for them of course they'd immediately see it our way and there'd be no problem. Unfortunately our children are not clones. They see things *their* way, and what we expect does not always go down well.

Often there's a compromise. Someone gives way or we reach an agreement. Other times we need to stick our toes in. If you have been burnishing your legitimate power there may be no problem. You will not need to use coercion. But sometimes legitimate power does not work either. Your child's wants or needs override their respect for you.

Threats and punishments are all coercive. You may need to use them. From your own experience you will know what works – and what doesn't.

At your wits' end

When we sink to beating, shouting, screaming, or crying we have to accept we have screwed up. These are last resorts, the fruit of frustration or exhaustion. Your coercive power isn't working – and the first thing to think about is why. Don't give yourself a hard time. Start instead to consider the job you're doing.

If you were in ordinary work, and were not your normal competent self, a sensible and efficient manager would suggest a few days off or perhaps a temporary transfer. Being a parent is not an ordinary job. What ordinary job goes on 24 hours a day, seven days a week? When you find yourself at the end of your tether, think about giving yourself a break.

We had for a year, a super Dutch au pair girl. She took care of our (then) two children when I went to work. She was great with the children and fitted in beautifully. When she had been with us about five months, we were washing up together one evening. Suddenly she dropped, and broke, a jug. Two days later she came to me, in tears, because she had broken another piece of china. Neither of these broken objects were of the least consequence. What concerned me was that breaking things was quite out of character for her, and so were tears. I suggested that she might like a short break back home in Holland. I got her a ticket, and when she returned from Amsterdam after five days' holiday she was refreshed and happy. It was no big deal. If someone was going to look after my children, that person had to be in good shape.

Being managers of ourselves

Parents do not have managers or supervisors – unfortunately. We rarely have someone to keep an eye on us, to make sure we are not overstretched. Often our partner (if we have one) is equally stretched, or sometimes simply doesn't notice. We have to keep an eye on ourselves – make sure we're not running down the batteries.

We need to be parents to ourselves, if we're going to be good parents to our children.

A decade ago, overstretched mothers trotted like lemmings into doctors' surgeries to get tranquillizers and anti-depressants when they were at the end of their tether. The whole of society was in the grip of the myth that a pill could solve any problem. Unfortunately the indiscriminate prescription of tranx created other, and sometimes more serious problems, as we now know. That door has been firmly shut. Chemicals do not solve management problems.

But many mothers do not have enough real life time off – and sometimes the pressure is kept up for years. If they are at work, their lunchtimes are filled with shopping, and they rush home to children and domestic duties. Holidays of course are spent with the children – either at home or away. Mothers who don't work are usually available to their children day and night. This is partly a consequence of the way we live today. Families are mobile. We shift around, making our little nuclear nests, often far from our extended families.

Delegate – spread the load

When I was young children used to spend a lot of holidays and weekends with aunts and uncles, grandparents, godparents, or other relatives. In consequence, parents got more natural breaks. Relatives are no longer so available. These days many relatives are working. People change their lifestyles more radically now-adays as the milestones of life go by. Above all, split families make it more difficult to invite relatives – families all too often have step-children to accommodate at weekends and in the holidays.

One of the unexpected bonuses for divorced parents can be the weekends or holidays or even the day-a-week that the children spend with the absent partner. Don't look this gift horse in the mouth. Although in some cases the child can be unsettled on returning to you, it is vital to make use of this valuable time to boost yourself up, to do something unexpectedly nice for yourself. You are not only being kind to yourself: if you are happy when your child returns, you are not going to put pressure on the child. Our children so desperately long for us to be happy – just as we would have them be.

No one is indispensable

When you know the pressure is getting to you, it's worth moving heaven and earth to get away for a day or two *on your own*. I can hear some of you saying, 'But how can they manage without me? How *could* I get away? Who will mind the children?' Nobody – not even a parent – is indispensible. Any moment any of us might be obliterated – and life would still go on. Just about any-one can manage to park a few children overnight if the chips are down. Use the energy you would put into fulfilling an urgent need of your child to organize a break for yourself. With or without a partner, a short rest from the children (i.e. your *work*!) when you are at frustration point is not a luxury – it is straightforward management sense. Keep it in mind. On ordinary good form you are not likely to abuse your coercive power. A young woman said to me, 'I was very frightened of my mother. She did not physically hurt me – but she was so stressed ... I was terrified by her rage and frustration.' Physical abuse of our coercive power is not the only indicator that we need to take stock. To do our job properly we need to take care of our stress levels.

Our coercive power is needed for our children's safety. But beyond the earliest stages, the best coercion is no coercion at all. If you can use any of your other powers instead, do.

When nothing seems to work

Most parents have a period when one child or another becomes impossible. But some families have a child who is particularly difficult – a child who appears to be impervious to all efforts at control. Little is said or written about such children, but parents who have one will recognize what I am saying.

If you are the luckless parent of a massively difficult child, you probably already have been to see one or more child psychologists. You have checked whether the child's frustration is due to being highly gifted. You have looked for signs of autism. You've wondered whether your child has some allergy which makes for emotional disturbance. If your child is physically and mentally 'normal', you will have ended up feeling extremely guilty – blaming yourself (and also your partner) for everything.

Nature – or nurture?

There are two ways – and only two ways – of looking at the problem. Either it is *nature* or it is *nurture*. The classic way society in general, and most professionals in particular, regard emotional disorders is this: if there is no sign of physical abnormality, then the cause has to be 'nurture'. By nurture, you can take it they mean parents.

Here are some of the standard explanations for emotional disturbance:

- The parents do not give the child enough love.
- The parents are inadequate: they do not know *how* to give their child enough love.

- The parents are emotionally disturbed/angry/rejected and project these emotions onto their child. Probably they are repeating an old family pattern.

- The father is jealous because the mother loves the child too much. Or vice versa.

- The mother is dominant, the father is weak. Or vice versa.

- The scapegoat theory offers an explanation in terms of family dynamics. This avoids specific blame and puts responsibility onto the whole family, which is now termed dysfunctional. In this scenario the 'difficult' child is seen as the emotional dustbin for everyone in the family.

If you have an extremely difficult child, you will agree that there could be another, much simpler, explanation. It is not impossible that your child was simply *born* with a contrary or obstinate or difficult personality. It might, after all, be not nurture, but nature. Anyone who has had two or more children knows that each child comes into the world furnished with entirely individual characteristics. No two siblings are alike. To an ordinary parent, a contrary child need be no more unlikely than a child with astygmatism. And just as by slow degrees astygmatism can be corrected, so too it is sometimes possible to redirect the contrary child's behaviour into more socially acceptable ways.

This explanation is no more – but no less – verifiable than any of the others, above. But it suggests practical, reality-based strategies, not the probing of old, and perhaps irrelevant, wounds. Parents who have to cope with difficult children *do not need* added guilt. They need support, and any techniques and skills that can help them to manage the daily grind and to get through *this day* with minimum turmoil.

Jane and Oliver had such a child. Louise had been a lovely, cherished baby, the youngest of four children. But from about two onwards she became difficult. She received as much attention as her older brother and sisters, but it never was enough for her. She was incessantly demanding, always wanting more than her share – of time, love, attention, whatever. She coaxed, nagged, whined, sulked, or screamed. When she wanted something she was relentlessly single-minded about getting it. She never gave in. She could not be shocked or shamed or punished into backing down. She discovered early how to manipulate the other five members of the family. Someone could always be manoeuvred into her service – and when she got what she wanted, she was all winning smiles and charm. In fact, as long as she got her own way, she could be a delightful child – warm, affectionate and lovable. But she was unpredictable. The only predictable thing about Louise was that if she wanted something, there would be no peace till she got it.

The parents talked endlessly about 'the problem with Louise', wondering not whether, but *where* they'd gone wrong. Oliver kept insisting that she'd get over it, that it was just a phase. Both parents kept hoping he was right. By the time Louise was seven her mother Jane had been on valium for a year and the parents had tried everything. They had been firm and consistent: and it hadn't worked. Both separately and together they had had quiet, thoughtful talks with the child: to no avail. They had used the silent treatment: but Louise could outlast everyone. If all else failed, she would enlist another member of the family. Her soft-hearted brother could always be counted on to plead on her behalf. If they shut her in her room she emerged smirking and unchastened. Jane started to smack her. Louise just giggled and said it didn't hurt. So Jane stopped it. Louise continued to manipulate the whole family and to create trouble. And now she was getting bad school reports. She was in a remedial reading class – though she was very intelligent.

Two years later Jane was told by a child psychologist that Louise felt herself to be unloved. If the child was given as much attention as she wanted, she would gradually ease off her demands. So Louise, (to the fury of her sisters and brother), was allowed to stay up with her parents, curled up night after night in front of the television until she dropped off to sleep. Oliver and Jane began showing serious signs of stress – their relationship was coming apart at the seams. They seemed to be quarrelling all the time. Jane finally made two major decisions: to come off valium and to send Louise to boarding school. She felt helpless to control Louise herself, felt that at a boarding school there must be a working system. Even if it didn't help Louise, which she prayed it would, at least the family would get a breathing space.

Jane told me all this much later, when Louise, now 22, was no longer living at home. Jane was very frank. She'd taken her daughter to several child psychologists and clinicians. There were various ways you could look at it, she knew. The most likely one was that Louise had been the family scapegoat. In that scenario, everyone in the family had focused their anger on Louise, rather than dealing with it. Louise colluded in this family game by acting out all their angry feelings for them. Jane's reservation about this picture was summed up in the question: *what had the family been doing with all their anger before Louise so conveniently turned up to focus it?* Her own view was that Louise's attitudes and behaviour had both sparked and fuelled a great deal of the family anger.

Jane also thought it possible that she or Oliver had failed to pull Louise up at a critical period of her development. Because she'd been so engaging and attractive, perhaps they'd let her get away with just one tantrum too many. She'd got the bit between her teeth and had hung on ever since. Secondly, Louise was a child of exceptional obstinacy and tenacity. Her emotional difficulties had begun as soon as she was old enough to relate to members of the family. Everyone who cared about Louise knew her to be like the little girl '. . . who had a little curl, Right in the middle of her forehead. When she was good she was very very good. But when she was bad she was horrid.'

On reflection, Jane thought it would have been helpful, would have enabled her to accept Louise and cope better, if there had been some kind of label for her. Thinking about the swathe of havoc Louise seemed to have cut through the family, the mother said it now seemed as if she'd been trying to bring up a handicapped child with no reference points and no proper support system. Louise was neither physically nor mentally handicapped but she *was* emotionally handicapped.

Jane saw herself as having failed Louise, despite all her efforts. All the 'help' she had approached seemed to imply that she – as mother – was largely 'to blame'. In consequence, her sense of guilt (shame) tripped her whenever she tried to get to grips with the reality of Louise's unacceptable behaviour.

Reality-based strategies

From discussions with Jane and other parents who have had the onerous task of bringing up a very difficult child, I have been able to elicit a number of suggestions which have been found to work:

1. **You do NOT have to accept unacceptable behaviour.**

2. **There is no occasion for guilt. NOBODY can be responsible for someone else's emotions, not even for your child's. You can only be responsible for your own emotions.**

3. Of course you have made mistakes. Everyone makes mistakes. But never forget that destiny or providence (or whatever name you choose) has a hand in everything. Who said YOU had to be omniscient?

4. The famous Serenity Prayer has supported millions of people in dire straits. Keep it in mind. It goes like this:

> God grant me the serenity
> To accept the things I cannot change,
> Courage to change the things I can –
> And the wisdom to know the difference.

5. Use the first two lines on your child, and apply the third line to yourself. Accept you cannot make your child change – but you CAN change yourself.

6. The way you can change is to detach. Practise taking your attention away from your child. Put your mind to anything and everything except your contrary child.

7. Practise not letting him or her press your buttons. Don't let yourself get upset. Remember 'this too will pass'.

8. Practise infinite courtesy with your child. Do not allow yourself to raise your voice, whatever the provocation. The 'Louises' of this world thrive on drama.

9. Be honest about your own shortcomings and wrongdoings. Apologize – properly – when you lose your temper, when you say something mean or petty or sarcastic – or when you do something wrong. THIS IS VITAL.

10. Find something nice to say to your difficult child EVERY DAY. Especially be generous with praise, approval and acceptance. Your reward power needs to be much in use – not for things, for strokes.

11. If you can find good professional help – either for yourself alone or for your child or for the whole family – take it. But bear in mind that if a parent-hunt gets under way, get out fast. You, after all, have to cope with the problem on a daily basis, and what you need is support.

12. The parents of very difficult children can get pretty

shell-shocked. Make sure you get some treats. You need them. Have a care for your own growth, mental and spiritual. You need all the care you can get. You need dreams and goals and ambitions and life-plans – and none of them to do with the children.

WITH A VERY CONTRARY CHILD, YOUR COERCIVE POWER WILL BE WELL NIGH USELESS. DON'T EVEN THINK OF IT.

REWARD POWER

'The first purpose of reward power is affirmation ... we all need to be affirmed and rewarded ... It is also essential for reinforcing good habits – and by its absence, to discourage bad behaviour'.

Affirming your child's self-worth

- rewards are powerful
- the greatest reward – your time
- the reward of responsibility

Affirming your own self-worth

- anxiety: enemy of self-worth
- some ancient wisdom to combat anxiety
- rewarding ourselves

Affirming your child's self-worth

The reward power of parents is a much bigger and more complex thing than it looks at first sight. It is not just sweets and treats for good behaviour: *rewards confirm and encourage actions and habits*. They tell your child loud and clear what you find acceptable and what you don't.

The first purpose of reward power is affirmation

We all need to be affirmed and rewarded. For new babies, being cradled with joy in a parent's arms is reward enough. Loving parents give this reward as a gesture of gratitude and delight in the baby's very existence. Rewards affirm our worth. They are the visible signs that we are acceptable to the people we love most on earth. Throughout the long days and short years of childhood we need constant recognition of our value.

Rewards are powerful

Rewards come in all shapes and sizes. The most effective cannot be bought over any counter: hugs, kisses, smiles, patting, stroking, verbal endearments. These are the very stuff of life. They are not only the first rewards, they are the best. A mother I knew was going through a really unpleasant time with a stroppy teenage son. For several weeks he was negative and uncooperative, and her best efforts at reaching him failed dismally. Their relationship had become distinctly strained. He avoided all communication. Finally she tried something different. One evening, as she passed the chair he was slumped in, she patted his shoulder in passing. Next day, again, she touched him lightly on the arm. Every day for a week she made a small, barely perceptible gesture that told him at a very deep level that he was acceptable as a human being. He was being rewarded, not for his behaviour but for his existence. By the seventh day he began to loosen up and gradually came out of his shell. Somewhere or other he had mislaid his self-worth – as we all can from time to time. In the simplest possible way she had discovered how to give it back to him.

Careless rewards backfire

The potency of our reward power is immense, and it requires us to make great use of common sense. Take the case of a baby of my acquaintance. When he was twelve months old this baby was being praised extravagantly because he had discovered how to twiddle the knobs on the television set and make the picture change. What a prodigy! 'Look at our clever baby! Do it again darling!' A few months later he was driving them mad by interfering with their viewing. Now they were having to stop him for doing what had previously been an occasion for praise – baffled baby!

Basic functions need no rewards

With reward power it is especially important to get your priorities right. Rewards can tell your child more about your priorities than you may wish them to know. Most people would agree that there are three primary needs which must, for life's sake, be met. They are food, disposal of waste and sleep. I've never yet known a parent to praise a child for having a good sleep, but I've heard hundreds (well, dozens) praise their child for 'eating up their dinner' or for sitting on a potty. Since both these activities are essential – and in the one case, enjoyable, in the other, a relief – praise is not only superfluous, it can be counter-productive.

When someone prepares a meal for me, I *thank* them. Perhaps if I knew it was a clever concoction of road sweepings and arsenic I might expect a word of *praise*, but I can think of no other reason.

It doesn't take a brilliant child to work out that if a parent is doling out praise for a pleasure, there's something else going on in the parent's head. And that something is just what the child can use when the child wants to make trouble, or to get special attention. Refusing to eat, making a fuss at mealtimes, has classic nuisance value. Just because it is such a high priority issue, it is vital the child doesn't find out.

I made lots of errors in bringing up my children, but I can be insufferably smug about the way they used to eat. They ate anything and everything. They were a pleasure to feed, and if other mothers didn't exactly line up to offer hospitality, at least the boys were always welcome at mealtimes.

There was nothing particularly clever about my system – but it worked. I simply assumed the boys would like what I gave them. If I made any exclamations, they were of the order of, 'There you are darling! Aren't you lucky?' or 'I'm cooking the most super supper tonight. Grilled fish and tomatoes – *with herbs*!'. Nobody got praised for eating. On the other hand, they never got food that I didn't enjoy myself. Since I'm not faddy, that meant just about everything. There were a few house-rules. They didn't have any chocolates or sweets until after they were three years old, and not many then. (These days they still hardly eat any). I kept no sweet biscuits in the house and there were no fizzy drinks except at parties. Between meals, the only option was fruit, juice, or milk. My youngest son showed some signs of faddiness so a new rule was added. Each boy could be excused from one thing only. Angus, the little one, chose peas. Andy chose eggs – which didn't always agree with him. And Alex, the eldest, chose chocolate pudding – on the principle that since he rarely got it anyway, he was unlikely to miss it.

We used to be amazed at some of the children who came to tea or to stay. This child wouldn't eat any green vegetables, that one never ate fish or cheese, the little schoolfriend staying for the weekend would only eat sugar puffs for breakfast – brought in his overnight bag with his pyjamas! Hardly any of them would eat salad of any kind. The trouble those mothers must have had with their children! And the wars! I'd love to say we never had wars, but I *can* say we never had them over food. Food – proper food – is so very important, I'm exceedingly glad my sons didn't discover what a powerful weapon they could have had.

Andy tried it *once*. He didn't feel like eating supper, he said, toying gloomily with his fork. He didn't feel well, he declared. I suspected there was some connection between his sudden loss of health and the fact that his brother had lately got a great deal of attention because of a fractured wrist. So I took him solicitously to bed, drew the blinds, and told him to try to sleep. He looked wide-eyed, as I prepared to depart. 'Aren't you going to stay and read to me, mummy?' he beseeched.

'Goodness me, no. If you're too ill to eat your dinner, you must be very unwell. What you need is rest and quiet in a darkened room,' I replied solemnly, and shut the door behind me. Five minutes later, miraculously restored to health, he rejoined the table and resumed his meal.

All the things which are essential to keeping life a going concern have their own built-in pleasure. Eating, defecating, passing water, sleeping – all these are their own reward.

On the other hand, food itself has all sorts of *responsible* reward possibilities. A special meal, a favourite dish, an exotic fruit – the options are endless because food is the only life-sustaining essential that is a genuinely shared and social pleasure. We do not share the lavatory. We may share a bed, but not sleep. But we do eat together.

For parents food provides extra fringe benefits. One of our given duties is to initiate our children into the great feasts of the year and to the family festivals. It is also our privilege to introduce them to the delights of the special occasion – the meal out, the summer picnic, the barbecue, the birthday party. We look forward together to the regular punctuation mark of Sunday brunch or Sunday dinner.

Rewarding your children

Reward power is what you are using when you give your children reassurance, when you are buttressing their sense of personal value. Giving them 'strokes' is the current way of describing it. As we saw much earlier, children no longer come into the world with built-in value in the way they used to, so parents need to use their reward power quite consciously, to make up the deficit.

The greatest reward – your time

Unquestionably the most valuable reward a child can receive is your time. Our consumerist society wants us to express our love in terms of 'things'. So parents often flog themselves to do extra work and overtime and part-time jobs to buy more and more of those 'things'. But 'things' break. Batteries run down. Toys are outgrown, discarded, and lost. Time you've spent happily with your child is stored in the deep treasure-house of the mind. It does not rust, nor does it decay.

Mind you, the operative word is *happily*. There's no point wasting your time or your child's by pretending you like baking pastry with the little darling if it bores you rigid. Children are no more taken in by being thrown sops than you are. Much better to do something that you'd enjoy doing, or need to do – and suggest the child join you. I learnt something novel just after Andy started in school. He'd never enjoyed nursery school and I hadn't insisted, but to real school he had to go.

About a week into term, as I collected him at the school gates, his teacher spoke to me, 'He's only a little boy, and I don't think it would matter if he missed an afternoon once a week for a while. He loves going to the supermarket with you . . . would you like to take him when you do the shopping? I think it would help him settle.'

I've heard some odd things in my day but that took the biscuit. But she was right, that teacher. A few weeks later, he felt affirmed and safe enough to stay happily at school full-time. Until then it had never occurred to me that our expeditions with a trolley were a highlight in his week. But it was extraordinarily valuable information. With blinding clarity, I realized that mundane things, done together, are of enormous importance. Thinking back I understood more.

Andy felt good because I appreciated his help in fetching the odd forgotten item – it pleased him to show off his memory – and his helpfulness. Because there were two of us, it wasn't so vile packing the bags and boxes, getting them into the boot, and out again at home. We achieved something tangible together doing what in the ordinary way I'd have thought only a rather irksome chore that had to be got through. Andy felt valued, because even at four and a half, he knew he could be useful. *He had a value.* And of course, doing things together cements friendships. Most of my close friends are people I've worked with in some way or other.

The reward of responsibility

Giving a child responsibility is a very effective stroke – and can dramatically transform a stroppy brat into a reliable human, as happened to Gail. Gail, now 12, was the younger of Barbara's two daughters. Rose, the elder, was rising 18. The whole family was planning a big 18th birthday party for Rose, and Gail, clearly very envious, was behaving obnoxiously. Rose was amused and delighted when her mother suggested that they decorate the whole house with masses of roses. She would order what they needed. It was too much for Gail. 'Roses are red, violets are blue, I think it's silly, Oh yes I do' she sang rudely, stuck her tongue out, and made for the door.

Suddenly inspired, Barbara gave Rose a warning glance and called Gail back. 'That's not very funny Gail, and I don't even think you believe it yourself. As a matter of fact I've been thinking. You're good with flowers . . . I thought you might take over all the arranging – if you'd like to.'

Stunned by this turn of events, Gail gulped. (Barbara later told me she looked as if she'd been chosen for *This Is Your Life*.) 'Do you really think I could?' 'I wouldn't have suggested it otherwise', said Barbara. In fact Gail did a beautiful and imaginative job; but more importantly, the opportunity for service, for responsibility, transformed her.

I have seen and heard of many examples of this kind of stroking. An aimless 16 year old who took pleasure at school only in his woodwork class was allowed to put up shelves in his parents' highly prized Georgian sitting room. The parents thought the boy's self-esteem was more valuable than the risk that he might do an unsatisfactory job. In fact I've never known a child to fail when parents have taken a calculated risk of this order. In some amazing way they always rise to the task. And the benefit from this kind of stroke flows outwards into all the child's behaviour.

Taking calculated risks on people is a prized skill in management: thus are talents are fostered. So too can it be in the family.

Reward power is primarily for parents to give their child affirmation. It is also essential for reinforcing good habits – and by its absence, to discourage bad behaviour.

Our cornucopia of rewards is huge. Not only do we have the whole array of hugs and kisses, pats and cuddles, praise and compliments, we also have the greater gifts of our time and our attention. We can bestow opportunities for responsibility and service. We can give presents and prizes and special treats. All parents have all this to give.

Isn't is surprising that many people – parents *and* children – have a frail sense of self-worth? Isn't it surprising that so many parents find it hard to discourage bad behaviour, with so many positive tools to hand?

Let's investigate.

Affirming your own self-worth

The recurring theme of this book is coming up again. *You can't give to someone else what you don't have yourself.*

We need a good sense of our own personal value if we are to affirm our children as they need to be affirmed, using our reward power for its primary purpose.

All of us suffer occasional drops in our sense of self-worth – set off by an unexpected reverse, a setback, an unfulfilled expectation. But others endure a chronic condition of low self-worth. You can almost measure your self-worth by your anxiety level. Anxiety flourishes when your self-worth is diminished.

In point of fact, anxiety is integral to the human condition. As far as we know, we are the only species that is aware of time – and of our own, inevitable death. We are therefore, each of us, heir to a fundamental anxiety about the meaning, purpose and value of our lives. Without purpose and meaning, perhaps there is only chaos? We all have to confront this issue. Our underlying and persistent anxiety is rooted in the dread of chaos. So it is that our continuing endeavour, as going human concerns, is to create order.

But to make the effort, we need to feel we have a value. In the beginning, this can only come from others. It is a fact that little babies, fed and cleaned, but not loved and valued, simply give up the ghost. They die. We must be affirmed, be given value, if we are not to give up the struggle.

Those of us who have got this far in life are survivors. Some of us may feel we did not get enough strokes, that we had a rotten background. But we're here. Our own parents may have given us little sense of self-worth. We may feel we were discounted and undervalued, or spoiled and misunderstood – but we made it, despite everything.

Even more importantly, we have the chance to control our own destiny. We are not hostages to our history. We can, if we choose, change direction. We cannot change the past but we can look at it from another perspective. And we can certainly change our attitudes and our behaviour so that the world, and the people around us, become aware that we are not to be trifled with. Our children can learn the invaluable lesson that it is *never* too late to change.

As parents, we have a job to do and we need to be fit for it. We have a primary duty to find ways and means to nourish our own sense of self-worth, and to overcome our anxiety. Let us look at what anxiety is about.

Anxiety – arch-enemy of self-worth

Anxious people are often obsessed with time. They are concerned about getting everything done, getting finished in time, fitting everything in. They worry about the future, agonize about the past. 'If only' and 'what if' are their unhappy mantras. Anxious men work grey and late. Anxious women dash between home and work, terrified that some great bell will toll and they will be found wanting.

Most anxious people are desperate for approval, but often they don't realize it. They are hard on themselves and the people they most love. They try too hard. They set themselves standards that are too high, and contradictorily, goals that are too low. They have little faith in themselves. They put themselves out for other people and hardly know why they are doing it. They agree to go places, see people, or do things, they don't want to do. They usually say it is 'for the sake of peace' – but that is not the real reason. Many parents – mothers in particular – who give in too much to their children, are really acting out their anxiety. They are scared of losing their children's approval. They equate love with approval.

Others are anxious to achieve – they put their work above all human concerns. These are often absentee fathers, who try to hide their personal absence with mega-presents. It is admiration they crave, mistakenly believing it to be love. Sometimes they even compete with their children, hoping that if they impress, they will be loved.

No seminars or training schemes

In many respects, being a parent and being a manager in the wider world are quite similar. But there is a great difference in the support services. Managers in industry, commerce, and institutions are continually being refreshed in their management skills, by means of courses, classes, seminars, and lectures. However, if one analyses the content of most courses, it can be seen that about 75 per cent of the material is concerned, not with how the manager handles other people, but how he or she handles him- or herself.

Some ancient wisdom to combat anxiety

Because the condition of anxiety has been with us since the dawn of time, wise people have always had ways to deal with it. These methods do not come wrapped in scientific languages or laid down in computer programs, so until recently, we have tended to ignore or forget them. But they work. They come from ancient, universal sources. Here are five which are particularly helpful for common problems of parents today:

1. **Take time.** Take it seriously. What time do we really have? We have this moment, *now* – and only this moment. We do not have yesterday and we cannot bank on tomorrow. The most we can reasonably plan for is what happens today. Live in this day only.

   Living life *in this day* gives us a sense of well-being. It compels detachment. Let us say you have a really tricky business matter to discuss tomorrow on the telephone. You know what you are going to say. You've gone over it in your head all day. You cannot make the call till tomorrow and in the normal way, you would brood over it sleeplessly all night. Now think again. Stand outside time and think about what is really possible. You can live in today only. Tomorrow may bring anything – or not even happen. You've decided the way you are going to handle the call. There is literally nothing you can do any more today, so put it aside and leave it there until the morning. You've done today's work. Tomorrow you will deal with tomorrow's work.

Living life just for today allows us to get our priorities in order. If this is to be my last day on earth (and who am I to say it is not?) I need to live it well.

2. **Slow down.** Anxiety speeds you up, creates panic. If you can find methods of grounding yourself, you can defeat your anxiety.

Here's a way to do physical work. Ever seen the way Japanese women work? Their hands are beautiful to watch. Moving quietly they make scrubbing saucepans into a work of art. The secret is to give your full attention – literally – to the job in hand, not planning the next thing while you rush through this one. The Buddhists put it simply: 'When we are sweeping the floor – we are sweeping the floor; when we are washing the dishes – we are washing the dishes.' Why this exercise should be so effective I do not know, but it centres you marvellously. Panic subsides.

Another way is to find your personal rhythm, and work to it. For this you need to listen carefully till you hear your heart beating. Then keep the beat in your mind's ear as you start your next job. Pace your movements to the measure of your heartbeat.

Run off your feet? Think about the way nuns glide along – they cover the ground, but the steady, even movement quiets an unquiet heart. When you're rushing around, trying to get to three places before they all shut, bring your mind back to the nuns. It will give you a pace without pressure.

3. **Think cosmic.** Frustration does not have to shatter your peace – not even that of being stuck in a traffic jam, or waiting in for a serviceman who hasn't turned up for the second day running. You cannot change circumstances, but you *can* change your point of view. For example, slow as it is, it's more comfortable sitting in a car than flogging along on foot. A couple of hundred years ago you would have been hoofing it. And isn't it more pleasant to have a machine to do the washing than having to boil coppers of water and heave the clothes out on a stick? In our grandmothers' time, the washing was done that way.

Secondly, you can try having trust in providence (or fate or what you will). While you are stuck here in this traffic jam (or kitchen or whatever) you are not rushing headlong into an accident. You are, perhaps, being kept safely in this boring jam to save you from a much nastier fate up ahead. It doesn't matter whether or not you believe in any kind of God or Super Intelligence running the universe. Your own intelligence will inform you that *all* experience can be *good* experience – whatever the appearance. There is always, without exception, some lesson you can take from everything that happens to you, good or bad. In this case you have just been having an exercise in patience. Don't be cross, be grateful.

4. **Act selfish.** If you are a dyed-in-the-wool people-pleaser, this is for you. You will find it hard at first, but stick at it. At least once this week refuse to do something you really don't want to do, something you are being pressed to do. Whether it is to empty the rubbish or prepare a late meal or simply to change the channel on the television, don't do it. Alternately, act out of character. Finish off the cream instead of skimping yourself. Use up as much hot water as you really need for a good bath, even if it does empty the tank. A friend practised this exercise, and happily reported that she had eaten the last of some special Belgian chocolates and . . . 'my daughter Maria actually said, "But mummy, you were *selfish*!"' That should be your aim. When one of your family accuses you of selfishness, you are getting there. The people around you will look at your with new eyes.

We create our own image. *We* decide, ourselves, how we shall be perceived. If we continually discount ourselves, why should other people bother to take account of us? The purpose of this exercise is to get you to experience the feeling of being important. It is specifically designed for people who are accustomed to put themselves second, or third, or last.

5. **Do yourself a favour.** We all have a number of aggravating little jobs that we keep putting off. A letter of complaint, a meeting to fix, some drawers to tidy, filing to sort, a toy to mend, a plant to move – low-profile things that hang about waiting to be done, never so urgent that they cannot be deferred, just a pain. Take on one of them on a bad day. I assure you, you will feel ridiculously good.

It seems to me that this works because by imposing order (in a small and practical way) we are fighting anxiety on our own terms. We are keeping a larger chaos at bay. Chaos cannot exist with order.

Rewarding ourselves

The job carries many built-in rewards for parents. They are mainly emotional, but the work of parenting is not only emotional. It is also physical and mental. That means from time to time, a shortfall. There is no senior director, no boss, no grateful client to give us a pat on the back, a bonus, or a pay-rise for doing a splendid job. Sometimes the work can *feel* unrewarding and everlasting. We can't exactly threaten to change firms, though I have to admit there were occasionally times when I thought wistfully about swapping my sons for another family!

Since we are both workers and managers, it is our duty from time to time to give ourselves rewards. Look over your work, your day, and assess it. If you have done well, acknowledge it. Just articulate it – to yourself. Make it a fact, rather than a vague thought. It makes being a good mother/father more likely tomorrow. It is, of course, an affirmation. Mothers who do not have another *paid* job can find it hard to spend money on themselves. Everything goes to the children or the household. It is imperative to ensure you also get a share of the goodies. How you do this, what you would like, is your own business – but do it.

To be effective in rewarding others, you need to know that you matter, that you have a real and tangible value.

Using these techniques as a basis, you can go on to strengthen your sense of self-worth. And from a strong basis you will be able to give your child the affirmation that this power requires. It's an affirmation of life itself.

MORAL POWER

'For your young child you express the entire moral system of its world because you are its world ... parents have to be seen to be responsible, to be accountable ... If we are to make full use of our Moral Power, we need to take regular stock of our lives as honestly and thoroughly as we can. We have then to be willing to change and to grow.'

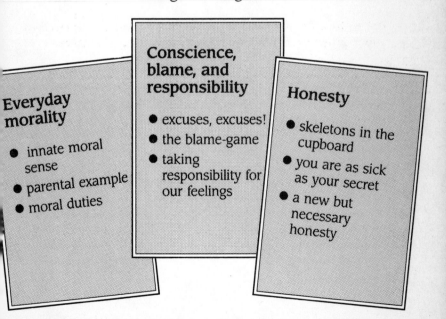

Everyday morality

- innate moral sense
- parental example
- moral duties

Conscience, blame, and responsibility

- excuses, excuses!
- the blame-game
- taking responsibility for our feelings

Honesty

- skeletons in the cupboard
- you are as sick as your secret
- a new but necessary honesty

Everyday morality

The importance of the parental powers changes as our children grow. As they become older, we have seen that biological, legitimate, coercive, and reward powers lose some of their punch. Moral power, on the contrary, becomes increasingly important.

This chapter is not going to be a dissertation on ethics. We're talking here about right and wrong, truth, honesty, fairness, and justice as we display these in everyday living.

For your young child you express the entire moral system of its world just because you are its world. Many people – not only the religious – have the conviction that we are all endowed from birth with conscience. In *The Child, the Family and the Outside World* Winnicot writes of 'the innate morality of the baby', and many psychologists recognize altruism and cooperation as primary characteristics of the species *homo sapiens*.

Innate moral sense

The fascinating fact is that even very young children have a fine understanding of many of these concepts. I was fortunate enough one Saturday morning to be allowed to sit in on a family 'court'. Victoria and Jerry, the parents, had never used corporal punishment, and had an interesting method of organizing rewards and punishments. The whole family was present for the hour it usually took.

There were four children, Nicky (9), Diana (7), Sophie (6), and

Oliver (4). During the week, the parents would give red or green marks to each child for bad or specially good behaviour and a tally was kept. At the court, the whole family contributed to the decisions. Green marks would cancel red ones.

This week they were starting with Sophie. She had five red marks and two green ones, making a total of three red. There was general agreement to Nicky's suggestion that since most of Sophie's red marks had come through laziness, her punishment should be to sweep all the garden paths.

Oliver had had a bad week. He'd collected seven red marks. 'I think he should forfeit most of his pocket money', said Sophie. 'No', said Nicky, 'He's got seven bad ones. He has to *do* something useful. What about bringing in the milk every morning for a week?' 'Dangerous', said Diana, 'he's too young – he might fall on them if he was in a hurry'. Sophie said thoughtfully, 'I think he should go to bed an hour early for a week. That would make him think.' 'Not fair', muttered Oliver mutinously. Everyone looked at him. He was rather pink in the face. Yes, early bedtime was a suitable punishment, the children agreed.

Nicky hadn't been all that virtuous. He had five red marks. 'I think he should do work for it', said Oliver promptly (no doubt getting his own back). He thought hard for a moment. 'I know! He can do all our jobs for the animals for a week – feeding them and washing their plates and everything!' 'It's an idea', said Diana doubtfully, 'but a week's too long for just five marks. Say three days? – together with his ordinary jobs that's enough.' 'No five', said Sophie. 'It's not all that hard, and he likes playing with the animals. A day for each mark.' They all agreed.

Diana had six red marks and three green ones. Like her sister, her final total was three red. The milk bottle chore was suggested for her. But Sophie's idea won favour. She proposed that Diana be stopped from watching her favourite television programmes for half the week.

What enthralled me was the seriousness with which the children approached this meeting, and the fairness they displayed. Their rewards and punishments were sensible and appropriate. The parents told me they'd only been doing this for a few months, but it had made a great difference. The children made sure that justice was done, and could be seen to be done. They took account of size and age quite naturally without any song and dance about it. They put a stop to any personal vendettas when it came to decision-making – and accepted their punishments without fuss. The hardest part was finding an hour during term-time when all the family could be together.

Justice and fairness, right and wrong, truth and honesty are on every child's agenda. We only have to think back and listen to the cry of the child we used to be: 'But it's not fair!' . . . 'He was wrong!' . . . 'She told a lie' . . . or perhaps. 'I didn't tell the truth'. We *knew* all right. From the very beginning we knew. And so too do our children.

For us parents, the time for talking is over. Centuries of parental hypocrisy have been swept away, and parents can no longer hope to get away with 'Do what I say, not what I do'. You will remember it was a child who shouted that the Emperor had no clothes? We need to make very sure that *we* are wearing clothes.

Parental example

Actions talk

It is not that our actions speak louder than our words: our actions effectively *are* our words. Parents who evade (or to put it politely, 'avoid') paying tax and other duties, who practise insider trading, who buy things that have fallen off lorries, who boast of cutting corners in business or who work on the black, can hardly be surprised if their children take to shoplifting. Parents who drink heavily can hardly be outraged if their children follow suit . . . although some youngsters may prefer other mood-altering drugs – cannabis, or cocaine, or heroin, for instance – rather than the legal drug, alcohol. Children naturally copy.

And inaction talks

We are weighed not only by our actions, but also by our lack of action. A father who permits a stepmother to maltreat his children has no defence against the facts.

Dougal was such a father. His second wife Alice was determined to alienate him from his two boys (who lived with their mother) in order to advance the cause of her own two girls (who lived with Dougal and her). When the boys visited, she made them uncomfortable and unwelcome. If a meal was in progress, there would sometimes not be enough for the visitors. *Her* daughters were not encouraged to share a room when Dougal's children stayed, so the boys had to bunk down in the sitting room – feeling unwanted, and in the way. They stayed less and less frequently.

The two boys were well aware that it was *their* father who paid the bills yet Alice contrived to make them feel like poor relations. *Her* daughters were not expected to do chores: the visiting children were expected to do the washing up. *Her* children got the best of everything, the boys were put down and discounted. Dougal pretended not to notice all the small but significant attacks on his children, and brushed aside any protests his sons tried to make. Although he was aware they were uncomfortable with his new wife, he perversely always insisted they come to his home, and Alice was always there. Perhaps he hoped propinquity would finally produce affection. He seemed to want them all to act out his fantasy world of Happy Families.

His sons perceived the whole scenario as a great betrayal. They could not understand why their father did not put a stop to Alice's undisguised ill-will. At 10 and 12 years old, they were unequipped to cope with her adult malice. They were, in any case, shattered by the break-up of their home and demoralized also by the relative poverty in which they now lived with their mother. The rock of paternal protection swept away, they foundered in a flood of insecurity.

This story is particularly interesting because of the obvious parallels with the archaic tale of Cinderella. When I asked about the attitude of Alice's children (the 'Ugly Sisters'), it appears that now and then one or other of them would make a small, embarrassed gesture of kindness or reconciliation, but in the main they reflected their mother's standards of self-seeking and material greed – thereby accurately, and surprisingly, endorsing the Cinderalla model.

Moral duties

At the extreme of inexcusable condonation is the parent (usually a mother) who knows her partner has assaulted her child – and who does not act. We hear a lot about fear these days. We hear little about cowardice. 'Sexual rivalry' sounds more clinical and less judgemental than its old name jealousy. But the opposite sides of these two coins, cowardice and jealousy, are courage and love. A parent who does not act in these circumstances has stifled all love. By not acting, she betrays herself, her child *and* the aggressor. If (as often happens) she carries her own shame because she herself was assaulted as a child, she now adds to it a dreadful burden of guilt, and the death of hope. However frightening the possible consequences, the parent of an abused child has no excuse not to act. *Fear is no excuse. You are responsible.* Make a start now.

How to act in some situations can be taxing. Bullying, for instance. If you know your child is being bullied, it is not responsible to do nothing. In this matter we need to exercise all the communications skills – particularly of listening – to find out as much as possible. Every situation is different – there is no one right action. Some parents have had success by taking the matter up with the school. Others have found it best to send the child to another school. Some have enrolled their children in martial arts classes. (Techniques of self-protection may not be the whole answer, but they can help.) *Parents who fail to act, fail their children – and fail in their moral duty.* Quaint words, aren't they? Moral duty is hardly a phrase that trips lightly off the tongue these days – but that's precisely what we are talking about.

Moral duty is linked to moral power.

Old problems – new solutions

With the disintegration of general social consensus, many alternative solutions have come into being to help parents in sticky situations. Advice centres and self-help groups exist today for almost any problem. Fifteen years ago there were no rape or incest centres of any size, and women's refuges were just beginning. There was no Families Anonymous to support the parent whose partner or child was drug dependent, little was known about the availability of Alcoholic Anonymous, Narcotics Anonymous, or Al-Anon (for the family member). There was no Parents' Anonymous for the parent who feared they might endanger a child. Some of these groups are action groups, some are support groups. Whatever you need, there's somebody in the community who can help. To find out where, most good local radio stations run a helpline and the Citizens Advice Bureaux are a great starting point. Two other resources are your local library and the Samaritans.

If your marriage or relationship is in disrepair, enlist the help of a marriage guidance counsellor. If your marriage is really on the rocks, and divorce is inevitable, you need no longer expect only bitter legal adversarial in-fighting – a whole range of Conciliation and Family Mediation services is now emerging, staffed by professional family counsellors and divorce lawyers. They are concerned with constructive problem-solving rather than confrontation, with settling difficulties amicably, and keeping the children's well-being especially in mind.

The existence of all these centres of help means we cannot camouflage our lack of action with any excuse of uniqueness. No iniquity, no pain, no problem, no injustice, is unique. There is certainly someone out there who shares your difficulty, and only sloth or indifference, cowardice or self-interest, is stopping you from making the effort to find them. Your initial telephone call is already a step on the road to recovery.

Unexpected bonuses from hardship

The remarkable thing is that when we act in the right way for the right reasons, the outcome is always beneficial. It may not seem so at first. 'Beneficial' does not rule out pain and hardship, at least for a time. But strength grows in proportion to the difficulty. It has been truly said that, 'We are never given a greater burden than we can carry in any one day.' Hang on to that when you hit a really hard place.

Yet even material hardship can produce odd perks. When Joanna left her husband because of his unacceptable behaviour, she and her children were cast into unaccustomed poverty. Parties, meals out, most treats, were quite off the agenda. Her eldest boy was philosophical, but the two younger girls were quite clear that being in straitened circumstances was not to their liking. For several months Joanna's difficulties were not helped by the girls, who moaned at intervals about how awful it was not having this and that and the other.

When her birthday was in prospect, unknown to Joanna the youngsters worked out a plan. They saved every penny they could, did extra jobs for neighbours, and booked a table in a splendid Greek restaurant for a celebration dinner. The restaurant was great. The owner discovered that the children were paying and added special treats (free). The zither player entertained them beyond the call of duty. They all had a euphoric evening.

As they left, one of the girls took Joanna's arm and said, 'You know mummy, there's something to be said for being poor, after all. Eating in a restaurant is a great deal more fun when you hardly ever do it.' Joanna felt that was quite the best present she received that birthday.

The important thing is to know that the right decision made for the right reasons may bring pain or hardship – but it will also bring unexpected gifts. The first gift will certainly be the knowledge that you can live comfortably with your decision. Moral Power does make big demands on us from time to time, but also – sooner or later – it brings its own serenity.

Conscience, blame and responsibility

Excuses, excuses!

The existence of a conscience might almost be deduced from the fact that everyone always wants to be *seen* to be in the right. People will go to extraordinary lengths to excuse behaviour that is plainly wrong: 'A momentary lapse', 'I was not myself', 'I was under pressure', 'Everyone does it', 'They asked for it' are classic justifications.

Paradoxically, moral power grows in tandem with our capacity to admit error.

'I'm sorry, I was wrong' is all that is required. But how rare, how exceeding rare that is! We fill the air with excuses, with alibis and with reasons, unaware that a simple admission of failure, error, or mistake is all that is needed. About 90 per cent of the time self-justifications are not justified.

Making justifications can even make things worse. When you have wronged someone and they are geared up for a massive scene, a straight, unqualified apology is completely disarming – excuses are likely to trigger off an avalanche. Watch it happening ...

> You: 'I'm really sorry but I've been under such stress lately –'
>
> Other: 'What stress? We're both under stress. But I can manage to get there on time. Why can't you? Trouble with

you is you never think ahead. You're always late, and this time you've really done it.'

You: 'That's simply not true and you know it. I've said I'm sorry. And anyway, you're a fine one to talk. The number of times you've kept me waiting. And what's more I wouldn't have been late if you'd fixed the car as you promised.' ... It can escalate indefinitely.

Any justification is likely to lead to a mighty conflagration because it broadens the field of dispute. But it takes two to play. You have a choice. If you really *are* in the wrong, why not just say so? What is wrong with being wrong? Who says you have to be right every time? You may have to put up with some of the other person's excess steam, but if you stick to your position and decline to excuse yourself, the threatened scene need not take place.

The blame-game

Then there is the great universal blame-game. This is the one which goes: 'I wouldn't have done it if you hadn't *made me* so angry' ... and 'Look what you *made me* do!' ... and ... 'He *made me* so upset I forgot what I was doing' ... and again ... 'It was all her fault, she kept pushing me and pushing me till I finally hit out.'

One of the most spectacular examples I heard was the man who telephoned his wife 40 miles away to ask her to come and pick him up from a hospital: 'Yes, I'm all right, but I had an accident. The car's a write-off. Yes of course I'm all right – just some scratches – but it was all your fault. You made me so angry on the phone, nagging about my drinking, I couldn't concentrate properly.'

Taking responsibility for our feelings

It may come as a surprise to learn that *nobody* can *make* us do anything. We are entirely responsible for our actions, and for our reactions.

Nobody can *make* you angry. You are in charge of your own emotions, and of your actions. We can *allow* other people to make us angry, we can allow our anger to be triggered by other people's words or behaviour, but the anger (or sadness or confusion or whatever) is our own.

Usually when we accuse people of 'making us angry' we are in fact angry with ourselves. The man in the car accident had every reason to be angry with himself. He had drunk more than he knew he should. He had wrecked a car. He'd landed in hospital. He had had to ask for help from someone who had questioned the wisdom of his drinking. He was angry all right. But the anger was his, against himself.

Blaming is a kind of self-justification, an evasion of responsibility. The proper, adult action of a full-grown parent is plain, ungarnished admission of error. If any 'but' clause is added, it effectively wipes out the apology. 'Yes I did it ... but you made me/but it's really your fault/but she upset me' – is no apology. It is opening the way for prolonged hostilities or for avoiding real amends.

Pretending to apologize

Pseudo-apologies are the very devil. These are apologies in which the words say one thing and the meaning is the opposite. The classic one is: 'All right, I'm sorry. It's all my fault again. I take all the blame, *as usual*.' Or, another classic, 'I certainly wouldn't want to hurt anyone but if you think I've hurt you, well I apologize'. In the late 1980s a very refined version began to appear: 'I certainly did not mean to offend you – if you *are* offended – that's *your* problem.'

The pseudo-apology is usually an expression of anger. It is almost screaming, 'All right, you can have your apology now, but just you wait till I throw the real lot at you'. Both parties know that there has been no real expression of regret and that nothing has been resolved, though the pseudo-apologizer may insist they've apologized. Tone of voice tells a lot. A real apology is whole-hearted and sorry. A grudging and resentful apology will not lay the matter to rest.

The unadorned apology

With children a simple apology is almost guaranteed to succeed. Most children abhor scenes and are only too delighted to get things cleared up quickly. They are graceful in understanding, generous with forgiveness. Give a child a plain apology and the child will probably fill in your alibis for you: 'That's all right Dad, I know you were tired.' They love to feel good. They are tender and tactful when a parent admits serious error, though over little mistakes they will probably make merry. Not much of a penance on the whole. They don't really expect you to be perfect all the time – do *you* need to?

The unexpected bonuses of taking responsibility

When you refrain from self-justification there are unexpected bonuses. First there is an exhilarating sense of a load being lifted. No hoops to go through, mustering your points and putting them across. No trying to make the blame stick. Since I can't make anyone else actually *do* anything, I avoid the frustration of trying to get them to agree that it's their fault I was angry. When I accept that my anger is my own, and the mistake was mine, at least I can do something constructive about it.

Apart from all else, how otherwise can we expect our children to admit their mistakes if we do not show them how? Honesty about our feelings is a new requirement. In the old days, when church and state and the whole of society maintained allegiance to the same straightforward moral code, parents were automatically given honour, respect and obedience. As we saw with Legitimate Power, these must now be earned – they no longer come with the job. A different quality of honesty and responsibility is now required of parents.

Parents have to be seen to be responsible. We have to be accountable for our errors and mistakes as well as our virtues. By the graceful admission of our fallibility we gain moral stature – and enhance our Moral Power quite surprisingly.

Honesty

Skeletons in the cupboard

Honesty comes in all sizes. We have so far been particularly concerned with honesty about our behaviour and our feelings. But there is a very different kind of honesty to take account of. That is *honesty about what is really going on*.

No family leads a charmed life for long. A major crisis or serious trouble of some sort is bound to happen from time to time in the best regulated families. A job loss, drug dependence, bankruptcy, divorce, a positive cancer test – there are hundreds of threatening situations, and no family escapes unscathed. Often the whole family will know about this – but sometimes it is decided to keep the matter secret from the children. It is worth thinking about this very carefully, and for reasons which almost certainly never occurred to our parents and grandparents.

First we need to acknowledge that all children listen on the stairs. Of course, children always have – if they could get away with it – especially when a secret might be discussed or a quarrel is simmering. The newer phenomenon (at least to me) is that most children have been through our personal effects. At the very least, sometime or other your child will have brought home a friend whose family ethos is somewhat laxer than yours – and a quick rummage will have been made through your drawers, wardrobe, cupboards, under your mattress, wherever. There's no point in being scandalized by this – but it is worth bearing in mind if you think you are hiding a secret. You probably aren't.

The Family Unconscious

More interestingly, there is a growing recognition that members of a family share a kind of common unconscious. It seems that all of us are to some extent aware of events and emotions in other members of our family that in the ordinary way should not be accessible to us.

My mother, a serious sceptic, told me about an event which had taken place when she was five years old. Her mother had been very ill for several weeks. One night the little child had a vivid dream in which her mother came to her, luminous and comforting. Then she said goodbye and floated upwards 'to heaven'. Next morning she was told that her mother had died in the night. A similar story was related by a friend in London. He woke one morning in great anxiety, having dreamed that his father had been in a fatal accident. He telephoned his home in Edinburgh and was immediately told that his uncle – his father's nearest brother – had died in the night.

Intimations through dreams of death and danger to family members are too frequent to be coincidental. Most of us have either experienced them, or known people who have done so. Various explanations have been offered of which telepathy is the most common. A recent theory advanced by Edward Taub-Bynum expands this simple label. Using rubrics which are available in quantum-relativistic theory, he suggests that the family operates in a kind of energy field, which he calls the Family Unconscious. He describes it as an 'enfolding web', in which family members share a rich treasure house of imagery and emotions.

One of the most flamboyant illustrations of the family unconscious at work is given by Jung. The three little daughters of a devoted mother each independently reported dreams in which their mother turned into a dangerous animal. Years later, their mother experienced a psychotic episode in which she got down on all fours and growled like an animal. The extraordinary thing is that unconsciously the children were aware, not only of their mother's underlying psychotic condition, but also of the exact way in which it would later manifest.

A survival mechanism

Aside from the likelihood of children knowing the unknowable (so to speak), there is a second consideration. The very existence of a baby or young child depends upon the adults in its life, upon their continued care and protection. The whole thrust of its being is bent upon observing and mobilizing important adults in its defence. To this end the young child is forever watchful, noting the fleeting smile, the suppressed frown, the quick inadvertent comment, eye-movements, body language – any subtle signs that give away information. It is, for children, essential work of self-preservation.

Now what are our children to make of all this miscellaneous and sometimes terrifying information? They process it as best they may, making what sense they can, or else they tuck it away – and from it sometimes grow dreams and nightmares, sometimes irrational fears and phobias. Of course it depends on what the information is.

By the time Henry and Sara's two young daughters were 9 and 11 their marriage was in serious disarray. Henry had a mistress – and not his first, there had been others before. Sara had borne with this for the children's sake – and because she was financially dependent on him while the children were small. Also, Henry was a loved and loving father.

But now the children were older, and for a year Sara had been running her own small business. She began to experience financial independence. Her own life began to look to her as shabby as Henry's. She had given Henry chance after chance, but he had broken all his promises and she at length decided that she could not much longer continue in a marriage so false, so lopsided – and so damaging to her.

For some months the younger daughter Josie had been reluctant to go to school. She invented excuses, dragged her feet, but went nonetheless. Sara was quite unprepared for a telephone call from the Head. Josie was really sick – she'd been throwing up in the washroom basin – and this was not the first time.

Sara kept Josie at home for a few days, and on the Saturday the balloon went up. Henry said he would be going out 'to a conference' and not returning until the Sunday afternoon. Sara told him to take all his things and not to return at all.

Comforting the children, trying to help their distress and deal with her own pain, she realized that both girls were aware of much more of the family trouble than Sara had any idea of. It became clear that Josie's school-sickness was her way of dealing with fear. The child had sensed danger to the family and felt she must be there at home to stop it happening. When it was brought out into the open and the real issues could be discussed, Josie was able to cry for her real loss, not walk in dread of half-formed demons.

You are as sick as your secret

Then there is Hannah. Hannah (aged 19) quite suddenly developed severe agoraphobia. There was considerable resistance from her parents when her friends urgently proposed professional help. There was no need to call in a psychiatrist or a therapist, was the response: the family could cope. Mummy would see her through. She would get over it.

But Hannah didn't get over it. On the contrary, her condition got worse. Proper, professional treatment became imperative. The therapist insisted on seeing both parents. Then, to forestall a bombshell, her mother broke 20 years' of silence and laid bare the family secret. Hannah's father was homosexual.

Once the secret was out, there was no further difficulty about therapy and Hannah's recovery progressed. Knowing the facts of her father's sexuality did not actually make any specific difference to Hannah's recovery, but the exposure of the 'secret' created a transformation. Hannah's mother also got professional help, and gradually, over time, the whole atmosphere at home began to lighten. To Hannah's amazement, a few months later it was possible even to laugh and make friendly, light-hearted jokes about her father's 'condition'. The whole family had begun to breathe the clean air of truth.

Hannah unconsciously chose a perfect vehicle to express the existence of a dark secret festering in the home. Her illness made it impossible for her to venture into the world. She must stay home and 'guard' the secret. The fact that *consciously* she did not know the secret was unimportant. The secret existed and it was grave and terrible. It had to be, did it not? Otherwise there would have been no secret. So she must be there to protect it. Here agoraphobia provided the cover.

It is said that you are as sick as your secret. It is also very likely that your children can become sick *because* of your secret. Whether the secret is that you yourself were assaulted as a child, or that there has been a lost job or promotion, the very fact of a secret is poisonous. A distinguished therapist says that keeping secrets disables all members of the family, whether or not they know the secret, 'because being secretive prevents the expression of questions, concern, and feelings (such as fear, anger, shame, and guilt). And the family thus cannot communicate freely.'

I'm not suggesting that you come right out and dump all your personal garbage here and now on your unwitting family. I'm suggesting that re-thinking needs to go on all the time. You could call it a reappraisal of the 'need to know' principle. The family is a system, interacting all the time at a dozen different levels. If a gear gets stuck, the whole system goes awry. In Hannah's family, something so crucial to the structure of the family as a parent's sexual orientation could hardly remain unnoticed at some level. Unquestionably, there had been opportunities much earlier for one or other of her parents to tell her. The sinister thing about secrets is that the longer they are kept, the harder it is to expose them. It takes great courage to face your child and tell your truth.

But the important thing to keep in mind is that when we do the thing we know in our gut to be right, only good flows from it. Hannah was in turns confused, distressed, and angry with her father – and furious with her mother – partly for living a lie, partly for not telling her. Bit by bit, over about a year, she talked it through, worked on it and came to terms with it. She is now closer to her parents than she has ever been. Oddly, now that it is no longer a secret, her father's sex life has become entirely his own business. Hannah can love and respect him as a person and as her father, because they can communicate without the dark shadow of the 'secret' lying between them.

A new but necessary honesty

This way of looking at the family is newly in the public domain. Of course children have always been much more aware than parents have ever given them credit for. The difference now is that the roof of social approval which convention once provided for parents – *just because they were parents* – has been shown up for the shabby leaky old tent it always was. We cannot any longer pay lip service to morality. We have to *be* moral. The way is much the same as the method we discussed for dealing with guilt.

If we are to make full use of our Moral Power, we need to take regular stock of our lives as honestly and as

thoroughly as we can. We have then to be willing to change and to grow. The great thing is that we can do this at any age. We can start the process any time. And through our changed attitudes, we automatically change the way we relate to our children. It is never too late.

I began using most of these techniques in my mid-forties – when my sons were already in their teens. A few years later, the following conversation took place as two of the boys were chatting about the mother of a friend. I asked idly, 'What's she like, Simon's mother?' Andy made a rueful face, 'Well – er – remember what you were like before you changed? About five years ago?' He grinned wickedly.

I've sometimes wistfully thought how much pain I would have been able to save myself and my family if I'd know when I was young what I know now. A singularly profitless line of thought. My parents would have had to know, and in turn *their* parents would have needed to know – and so on back through the generations, till Adam and Eve, no doubt.

Parents are gods

Our moral power derives directly from the fact that to babies and very young children, parents are gods. They have no other. Gods can do no wrong. Therefore if our gods perpetrate wicked deeds, if they inflict wounds on our minds and bodies, it follows that we must have deserved it. If our gods lie and cheat and deceive, gods cannot be wrong, so it follows that the 'wrong' must be in ourselves: *we* must be wrong, *we* must be bad. This happened to many of us when we were children ourselves – but we do not have to visit it on our own children.

We can stop the rot right here. Humans are infinitely adaptable. We can choose to take a new look at our life, we can decide to open up dark cupboards and throw light onto dank evil secrets. No question, it *does* take a great deal of courage – but the beautiful thing is that when we act in the right time, in the right way, and for the right reason, the rewards are out of all proportion to the pain.

As our children grow up and take over their own lives, our immediate usefulness to them diminishes – as does the practical application of most of our parental powers. But

our Moral Power never fails.

We accumulate experience throughout our lives – through our decisions, dilemmas, achievements, disasters, successes, mistakes, and recoveries. Nothing new there. Everyone gets experience: but not everyone gets wise. Wisdom is something else. The root of wisdom is Moral Power – and of what use are the elders if they are not wise?

PERSONAL POWER

'In the end what matters is not what we do for our children, but who we are for them.'

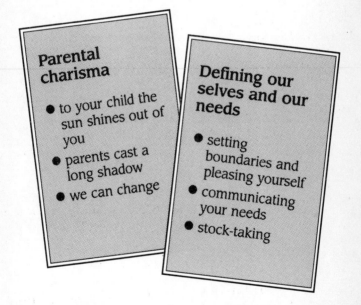

Parental charisma

- to your child the sun shines out of you
- parents cast a long shadow
- we can change

Defining our selves and our needs

- setting boundaries and pleasing yourself
- communicating your needs
- stock-taking

Parental charisma

You may not think of yourself as a charismatic person, but to your young child you have all the charisma in the world. The sun shines out of you. You *are* your baby's world.

Babies – and new parents – have no other reference points. I recall with some amusement how I felt after my first child was born. I never tired of looking at him. He was quite, quite perfect in my besotted eyes. When I saw other babies I found myself regarding them in astonishment, even dismay. How odd that one looks! What a *plain* child! That's not at all what a baby should look like! Any child who didn't have the huge forehead, round bald head and big blue eyes of my baby was much to be pitied.

In time this total maternal obsession diminished – but I have to admit, when my second child appeared with a totally different appearance, I was temporarily nonplussed. He had delicious soft curls, a long elegant head and even bigger blue eyes. I called him my surprise baby – and then, for a time, he in turn (like his brother after him) became the perfect example of what all 'proper' babies should look like.

Parents cast a long shadow

But whereas parents can and usually do have more than one baby, babies never have more than one mother and one father. Or at the very least, one primary caretaker. And the primitive devotion and enthusiasm inspired by the person of the parent always remains in the child's heart. One's own parents are – in a sense – always the very pattern, the Platonic form, of a parent.

Whatever you do, however you behave, some of this magic will always be invested in you. You will always be a presence in your child's life, just as your own parents, living or dead, are always a presence in *your* life. Parents cast a long shadow.

Considering it this way, it is easy to understand why it is so essential for us to take care of ourselves, to be aware of and responsible for our attitudes and behaviour. These tell our child everything about us. Children may be too kind or too afraid to comment, but information about us is continuously, if unconsciously, recorded. We must face the enormous truth that in our ordinary, everyday life we are making history, our children's history.

In the end it is *who we are* that matters. Not what we *do* for our children, but who we *are* for them. Charisma resides in our person. The part of our parenting job which most easily gets overlooked today is being a model for our children. We are so besieged with things we 'should' *do* or *buy* for them that we do not always remember this vital fact.

Quite a lot of people – (parents!) – carry the curious idea that their personality and character is set in concrete, particularly when it concerns the less attractive traits: 'I'm lazy – I've always been – it's the way I am' or 'I've got a terrible temper – always did have'. Sometimes this comes from being labelled by others in the past, sometimes it is a personal trademark we flaunt because it allows us to go on being lazy or bad-tempered. 'That's the way I am, take me or leave me' or 'I've always been like that – I can't change the way I am' is a cheap way to nurse the nasty bits of ourselves.

It is also totally untrue. *We can change* ourselves in every important way – and it does not necessarily take a vast amount of time. The only thing in heaven or earth we have real control over is ourselves. *We can change* our attitudes and our behaviour. We do not have to live our lives at the mercy of our personal past. We do not have to be automata, letting other people press our buttons. *We can take charge of our lives*. We can surprise even ourselves.

Defining our selves and our needs

For a large part of my life I actually didn't know who I was. If I confided in someone that I was nervous about going in late to a roomful of people and I was told 'Just be yourself!' I was absolutely no wiser. I lived my life in a series of masks and in those days I had to know exactly what mask to wear.

Later, after I had begun the process of finding out who I really was, I discovered to my surprise that I was not by any means the only person who felt the way I did. Far from being the only insecure, frightened, self-conscious person in the world – as I had grandiosly supposed – I found that a great many people, a great many other *parents*, have exactly the same difficulty.

Pleasing yourself

At the beginning, it was not useful to work from the basis: 'what makes me most comfortable now' – but rather: 'what will make me least uncomfortable in the longer run'.

Let me illustrate. Say it's Saturday night and I'm really tired. I've had a hell of a day, and all I want is an early night. My partner (or parent or child or friend) is dead keen to catch a movie which is only showing that night. I explain I don't want to go: I am exhausted. If I listen carefully, I'll hear in my voice a note of hesitation – deference/appeal? Of course the other person latches on to that thread of doubt: '*Do* come. It will do you good . . . get you out of yourself, make you laugh . . . it's only on tonight . . . it won't be the same without you . . .' – things like that.

What course of action will make me *most comfortable*? Either.

149

I would be comfortable going to bed early: and I would also be comfortable following my usual pattern of giving in to another person's demands/requests/manipulation. I would be comfortable *people-pleasing* because it's something I know all about. If I don't do what the other person wants – (and wants so much more definitely and insistently than I do *not* want) – then they will be displeased with me ... be angry ... love me less ... think I am selfish ... have cause to *criticize* me.

So what will make me *least uncomfortable* in the longer run? If I give in, I will probably feel physically weary, and wearier still in the morning, even if I do enjoy the film. More importantly, I will sink even lower in my self-esteem. Once more I have allowed my boundaries to be breached. I have taken the course of least resistance. Inside me yet another niggle adds itself to the pile of resentment which is really my own stuff. Sometime, somewhere, I shall blow. The next time we have a problem I may well accuse the other person of 'selfishness and lack of caring'. I might even be right. They might really be selfish and uncaring – but I am an adult human being and in charge of my own needs. If I cannot state them plainly and ensure that they are met, then that's *my* problem – and only I can deal with it. *I do not have to comply with other people's demands when they infringe upon my personal needs*.

Doing the right thing for myself hinges entirely on an internal decision. Once I make that decision (in this case not to go) it becomes unexpectedly easy. My 'self' does it all for me. In a firm but pleasant voice, I can hear myself saying, 'No – sorry, I am not going out tonight. I'm going to bed'. There are no hidden 'ifs' or 'buts'. I'm not apologizing or excusing myself or trying to give an explanation. I'm not going out and it's no big deal.

Of course the other person may be disappointed, angry, sulky. They may stay home and huff. But if they behave badly *it is their problem*, not mine. If they choose not to go to the movies, *that is their choice*, not mine. If they choose to be disappointed simply because I do not wish to go – tough!

Setting boundaries

The important thing for me is that I have made a start on consciously defining my boundaries. I have taken a big step towards changing my self-image, towards improving my own sense of self-esteem. And the process is cumulative. When I do what is right for me, inside, I begin to feel better about myself. Setting boundaries, bit by bit, eventually enables me to find out what I like and what I don't like – and in time, who I really am.

As a responsible parent, it is vital I set and keep my own boundaries – otherwise my children will grow up not knowing how important boundaries are. They too will give in when it is not good for them – not knowing any better. They too will pillage other people's boundaries.

With weak boundaries we submit to invasion. We also fail to respect other people's boundaries. We try to manage and control the whole world – or at least our corner of it. Of course, to do that, we have to be everywhere at once. It is exhausting – and aren't people ungrateful? They simply don't understand how well *we* could manage *their* life if only they'd let us. They carry on doing what they want, whatever we tell them. We might as well have saved our breath.

Indeed and we might, too. I have to confess I speak from personal experience. But being a parent does not give us rights to invade our children's boundaries. One of the most important (and humbling) lessons I have had to learn was to *mind my own business*. Alex – at 15 – came home one day with a wicked grin and a present. It was a 17th-century Nun's Prayer. It starts:

Lord. Thou knowest better than I know myself that I am growing older and will some day be old. Keep me from the fatal habit of thinking I must say something on every subject and on every occasion. Release me from craving to straighten out everybody's affairs ... With my vast store of wisdom it seems a pity not to use it all – but thou knowest Lord that I want a few friends at the end.

(Historical Reproduction Group, Cirencester, England.)

The more we work on our own boundaries, the less time (and temptation) we have to interfere with other people's – including our children's. I keep the Nun's Prayer in a prominent position. (Thanks Alex!)

Our personal space

Boundaries also involve space. We each need privacy. A slice of time apart and alone. Our needs vary. Some people need a lot, some a little – but don't kid yourself you need none. If you are uneasily aware that your partner and your children are always in your pocket, if you sometimes feel stifled or crowded, don't ignore the feeling. Do something.

When a baby is very new, the mother specially needs to take time for herself. In our western culture a baby does not confer a special virtue on the new mother: in most eastern and middle eastern countries the state of being a mother is revered. In the west, the baby itself is supposed to be gift enough for the mother – yet new babies can often be as much trauma as treasure. Since our society is not given to cherishing new mothers – 'Well, she *wanted* it, didn't she?' – you must cherish yourself as well as the new baby. Carve out a small sliver of time for yourself each day. You'll be a better mother because of it.

Boundaries involve not letting yourself be used up by one and all. The good mother, the good partner, the kind friend who is always there, also needs to refuel. We can overload the boundaries. When we're tired, we need to have the courage to say 'enough' – and the humility to lay our weary head on someone else's shoulder. We have to stop being the great giver. We have to hand that privilege to others in our turn, and accept our human frailty.

The 'ought-istic' bully within

'I *ought* to go and see ...'

'I *should* really do ...'

'I *must* be ready to ...'

Who says so? What is this 'ought-istic' voice that nags away internally all the time? We are adults, are we not? So what can we do about it?

Some years ago I became aware of how dominated I was by this internal bully. As an experiment, I decided to scrap the phrases, 'I ought', 'I should' and 'I must', from my vocabulary for a month. I would replace them with, 'I want', 'I intend', or 'I have agreed'.

Let me tell you it was one of the most difficult things I've ever done. I was shocked to discover how often I used those dire phrases and how much they masked my true needs. During that time I found out a great deal about what I liked doing and what I hated. It helped me to put a stop to some self-defeating actions

– things I went on doing out of some archaic and misplaced sense of 'duty' which was totally unrealistic in terms of my present life. I'd better confess here and now that I could only keep it up full-time for about 10 days. But it was a marvellous exercise that led to many surprises. Even doing it from time to time will tell you a lot.

Communicating your needs

Don't rely on telepathy

A great many of us find it very difficult to state our needs. We expect people to know by telepathy what we are feeling. It is very difficult, if you aren't used to it, to say, unequivocally, 'I feel uncomfortable/ sad/ frightened/ lonely/ abandoned/ rejected/ angry.' And so on.

This is partly because in our society, we all breach each other's boundaries, giving and taking blame for each other's emotions as we have discussed earlier. Yet there *is* a way – and the secret lies in the way we say it. The trick is to avoid laying blame. When I report an emotion, I am not making a judgement on the emotion, nor am I attributing blame. I am simply saying, 'This has happened to me. This is what I am feeling.' Here are a few non-blaming starts to practise with:

'*I know it's my problem*, but when you tell me you don't want me to come with you, I feel very abandoned.'

'*I don't know why it bothers me*, but when you talk like that I feel frightened.'

'*Maybe I'm being hypersensitive*, but that remark makes me feel angry.'

'*Perhaps I am overtired* but this discussion is making me feel uncomfortable.'

Most people find it much easier to report emotions in the past – emotions that have come and gone – than to admit to feelings here and now. But only if we report them *now* can the people we are with respond appropriately. We cannot, in fairness, expect them to know by telepathy or to have X-ray eyes. And furthermore, as soon as we do say what we are feeling, already some of the sting disappears.

By the same token, we cannot know what others are feeling unless they tell us. Several times I have gone to great lengths to comfort a partner or a child because of something that happened to them – only to discover (rather embarrassingly) that they weren't in the least upset by the incident. The things that upset me are not necessarily the things that upset the people I love. And vice versa. Telepathy is a very faulty medium of communication: honest words work a great deal better.

Being heard

When we were considering dynastic power, we talked about listening to our children. Being heard, being listened to, is a universal human need. When I feel that I am being truly heard, I begin to know who I really am. *Do not do all the listening: make sure that you, too, are heard*. If it cannot be managed inside the family, find a friend or a counsellor or a priest or anyone you feel safe with, and begin to open up. This is essential for your interior health. Most of us are frightened when we first start. What will I find? Will they be disgusted that I am not always loving, and forgiving, and grateful, and *good*? Let me once and for all put your mind at rest – nobody, but nobody, is all those wonderful things.

Some years ago I was part of a small self-help group. About eight of us needed somewhere to 'dump'. There were two Anglican priests, a probation officer, a couple of counsellors, a headmistress of a school, and me. Once a month we met for the whole day, and in rotation each one led the group. In every meeting different stresses surfaced – but we all shared our anguish of rejection, anger, resentment, abandonment, guilt, shame. We spoke and we were heard. We were heard without criticism or judgement. We were accepted and supported, warts and all. After the meeting we made sure that there was lots of comfort and hugging and we always had a meal together, sharing food as we had shared pain. The reason for mentioning this story is to underline the fact that everyone, but *everyone*, suffers all the 'negative' emotions – and we all have to share them to shed them. If we don't they will bring us to our knees.

Stock-taking

To enhance our Personal Power, we have looked at a number of ways to get in touch with our own feelings and needs. These have mainly been skills and strategies to use in everyday transactions.

We will now consider a procedure which is commonplace in practically every other department of working life – stock-taking. Schools have reports, colleges have assessments, firms have audits, businesses take stock. Every going concern makes a record of assets and liabilities, of achievements and deficits, profit and loss.

Let us consider the kind of stock-taking parents could do – and why. It is a writing job. And ideally it begins with the story of your life. If you haven't considered this before, it may sound an outrageous idea. Actually it can be – and usually is – transforming. The purpose is to find out what you've got to work with, and to clean up some accumulated lumber in the attics and cellars.

Starting with the first memories you have, write down all that you can remember up to today. The point is to find out the events and emotions which have most shaped you. When you are writing, put down all the things, however small or petty or shaming, however big and traumatic or devastating, that have befallen you. Try to re-feel your emotions and put them down on paper. You may find yourself in tears or in fury. When you were a child many things certainly happened that caused you strong emotions – often anger or pain or shame. Just keep writing. These things happened – and putting them down in black and white in a curious way exorcizes their power. It is cathartic.

The second reason for writing your Life Story is that when you finally come to read it through, you will almost certainly find that you have been repeating certain patterns of behaviour. You may see (for instance) that you consistently chose friends who left you in the lurch, or perhaps you always did the rejecting (getting in first, perhaps?) If you were painfully teased when you were a child, you will seem to attract putdowns and hurtful sarcasm even in your adult life. When it's all down on paper a great deal becomes clear.

You will also be able to see where you have been unkind and unfair, where you have been motivated by fear or anger or pride. Or by envy rather than by goodwill, by self-interest rather than generosity, by greed rather than love. When your life is laid out in black and white before you, it is hard to avoid some home-truths. This way you can learn the things to be careful about, the things that you need to work at if life is to be really comfortable and easy.

You may still wonder whether this isn't it an unnecessary self-indulgence? Scratching round in the past – well, it's gone, hasn't it? True, it's gone, but we contain our past in our present. Our past is always in some way part of us. We can ignore it, or we can use it. If we ignore it, if we haven't properly assimilated and come to terms with former wrongs and pain, they can lie in wait and leap out unexpectedly in moments of pressure or distress. To use our past properly, we have to see it for what it is. If we have not forgiven ourselves or the people who have hurt us, we will continue to be angry or vengeful or depressed even when there is no good reason for these feelings.

When we see our patterns, we can do something about them. If we do this job carefully, we will put power back in our lives. We can be free of old patterns. When a situation arises that we know is really part of an old pattern, we can choose not to repeat it. We are *not* at the mercy of a whimsical fate. We can control the events that happen to us here and now, today. We are only at the mercy of people and places and things when we do not know any better. Writing our Life Story is a key to power over ourselves because it helps us to know ourselves better. In very truth knowledge is power.

If it seems too tall an order to do your whole life in one go, do it in bits. Start with your first seven years. Then perhaps you might want to look at your relationship with your partner or your children. Or with one of your children. Keep the story on yourself and your own reactions – not on the other person. Chronology is not important. What *are* important are *your* feelings and emotional responses.

You will find that having made a start on this personal stock-taking, you will have a reliable tool to fall back on at any time when the going gets rough. When crises occur (and nobody is immune) you can get an unparalleled relief and perspective – and uplift – from writing it all down, including your feelings and your deepest motives. The more ruthless you are with yourself, the more benefit you get from it.

Bear in mind at all times the tough but undeniable truth that, 'it is a spiritual axiom that every time we are disturbed, no matter what the cause, there is something wrong with *us*'.

After you have done your Life Story, there is a further step you may decide to take. If you know someone who is wise and trustworthy (*and not directly involved in your life*) you could ask them to go through it with you. This takes courage. But if you choose someone with experience and love and good sense, you will gain immeasurably. Having your 'terrible' secrets accepted *without criticism and judgement*, having your difficulties acknowledged as human frailties which are common to us all, is a tremendous relief. And another perspective on your dilemmas and difficulties can be illuminating. But if you don't know anyone suitable yet, don't rush in. You will find the right person when the time is right.

Let's sum up. As parents we automatically assume a luminous charisma for our children. We cannot shed it any more than we can shed our own shadow. But if we don't like its shape or colour, there's nothing but ourselves to stop us changing it. It's a matter of changing ourselves, and *that* is very much our own business.

The job description

Our rights and our responsibilities

Resource: BIOLOGICAL POWER

Responsibilities:

- To protect my children and to provide for them the life-sustaining essentials they cannot provide for themselves.
- To help them learn how to take over these tasks and develop as independent people in their own right.
- To make the house rules.

Rights:

- To be wrong, to make mistakes.
- To have my personal space and time. Not to be always and instantly available.
- To be selfish – to protect and value my own needs.
- To have the house rules observed.

Resource: LEGITIMATE POWER

Responsibilities:

- To receive respect from my children.
- To give my children the security of limits and ensure they are kept.

- To teach my children, by example, how to deal responsibly with their feelings – particularly negative ones.

- To take responsibility for my own mistakes and wrong-doing, thereby building my own self-respect.

- To say NO and make it stick.

Rights:

- To be respected.

- To have negative feelings.

- To decline to give reasons for a decision.

- To change my mind.

- To say NO.

Resource: DYNASTIC POWER

Responsibilities:

- To hand on my skills, knowledge and wisdom to my children.

- To create opportunities for them to develop their full potential.

- To check my motives before opening doors for my child.

- To offer my children the best of myself – remembering that we are always making history: family history.

- To share *myself* with my children – by listening and communicating – and showing them how to do likewise.

- To play games, make music together, and tell them stories.

Rights:

- I have the right to decide whether (or not) to open doors for my child.

Bonuses!

- Singing ... storytelling ... playing games ... need one say more?

Resource: COERCIVE POWER

Responsibilities:

- To care for my children enough to control them.
- To act, talk, and behave without hypocrisy – not expecting my children to do what I say but what I do.
- To try to get my priorities right.
- To treat my job *as* a job – and when I am overstretched, to do something concrete about it, such as delegating.
- To acknowledge that no one is indispensible – not even me!

Rights:

- To know better than my child on many issues.
- To refuse to accept unacceptable behaviour.
- To refuse to take responsibility for anyone else's emotions – even my child's.

Resource: REWARD POWER

Responsibilities:

- To think carefully about the rewards I use and the way I use them.
- To use rewards responsibly to confirm good habits and to discourage bad behaviour.
- To give my child the greatest reward in the world – my time.
- To consider new and creative rewards – such as giving my child special jobs or responsibilities.
- To remember that the ultimate reward for my child is affirmation of its very existence.
- To build up my own self-worth, using every technique I can find.

Rights:

- To give myself proper rewards – remember I am the boss as well as the worker!

- To affirm myself.

Resource: MORAL POWER

Responsibilities:

- To recognize that what I do *always* matters. Children learn by copying.
- To remember that what I don't do also matters.
- To apologize when I am wrong – without 'buts'.
- To stop the blame-game (especially my own part in it!).
- To take responsibility for my own feelings – they are no one else's fault.
- To try to do the right thing at the right time and for the right reason – and not expect to control the outcome.

Rights:

- To make mistakes and not to need excuses.
- To have and to express my feelings and beliefs.
- To make my own decisions.

Bonus!

- A burnished conscience and a much more comfortable life.

Resource: PERSONAL POWER

Responsibilities:

- To remember that it is more important to *be* things for my child than to do or buy things for them.
- To change. It is never too late. (Unless, of course, I am now perfect.)
- To set and keep my own boundaries, to teach my children to do likewise – and also to respect other people's boundaries.
- To make sure I am being heard – that I am not merely the universal listener.

- To try to diminish the 'oughts' and 'shoulds' and 'musts' in my speech and my life, for they diminish me.
- To take regular stock of my life and my work.

Rights:

- I have the right to change.
- And to set my own boundaries.
- I have the right to be heard.
- And not to be taken for granted.
- To discover and to meet my own needs.
- To do what is *right for me*, in the certainty that this is always going to be best for my children.

Helpful resources

If you don't know where to turn for help, good places to start are your local library, your local radio station (which often has an advice or help line) or the agony aunt/uncle on a newspaper or periodical. All these normally keep a fairly comprehensive list of organizations both professional and self-help. The short list here should give you an idea of how many different kinds of organizations exist. You could ask them to suggest a possible alternative agency if they cannot themselves give you the help you need.

Some of these numbers have 24-hour helplines, but it is generally better to telephone in office hours. If you write, send a self-addressed, stamped envelope.

UK

Al-Anon Family Groups,
61 Great Dover Street,
London SE1 4YF.
Tel: 071 403 0888.

(*Self-help groups for families of people with a drink problem*)

Alcoholics Anonymous,
PO Box 1,
Stonebow House,
Stonebow,
York YO1 2NJ
Tel: 0904 644026.
London: Tel: 071 352 3001 (find local numbers in telephone directory)

(*Self-help groups for people with a drink problem*)

Association for Post Natal Illness,
7 Grosvenor Avenue,
London SW6 6RH.

(*Nationwide support scheme*)

Autistic Society of Great Britain,
276 Willesden Lane,
London NW2 5RB.
Tel: 081 451 1114.

Beaumont Society,
BM Box 3084,
Camden,
London WC1N 3XX.

(*Help for transvestites*)

British Association for Counselling,
37a Sheep Street,
Rugby, Warwickshire CU21 3BX.
Tel: 0788 78328.

(*National body giving information about local counselling services and individual counsellors*)

CAB
Citizens Advice Bureaux
see local directories

(*Free information, help and advice on all legal, social and personal matters: including welfare rights, housing, employment, consumer issues, financial problems etc*)

Childline
0800 1111

Compassionate Friends,
141 Lower Paddock Road,
Oxhey,
Watford WD1 4DU.
Tel: 0923 224279.

(*Advice, support for parents who have lost a child*)

COPE (UK) Prevention of Family Strain and COPE Family Groups,
68 Charlton Street,
London NW1 1JR.
Tel: 071 278 7048.

(*Help on all family issues*)

CRUSE
National Organization for the Widowed and their Children.
Cruse House,
126 Sheen Road,
Richmond
Surrey TW9 1VR.
Tel: 081 940 4818.

(*Advice, support for the widowed and their children*)

Depressives Anonymous,
36 Chestnut Avenue,
Beverley, North Humberside HU17 9QU.
Tel: 0482 860619.

(*Provides contacts with self-help groups dealing with depression*)

Divorce Conciliation Advisory Service,
38 Ebury Street,
London SW1W 0LU.
Tel: 071 730 2422.

(*Advice and practical help for divorced or separating parents*)

Families Anonymous,
310 Finchley Road,
London NW3 7AG.
Tel: 071 431 3536/071 731 8060.

(*Self-help groups for families of someone with a current, suspected or former drug problem*)

Families Need Fathers,
37 Garden Road,
Southwark,
London SE15 3UB.
Tel: 071 639 5362.

(*To maintain a child's relationship with both its parents after separation or divorce*)

Family Service Units,
207 Marylebone Road,
London NW1 5QP.
Tel: 071 402 5175.

(*Aims to prevent breakdown of family and community life by providing services*)

Gingerbread,
35 Wellington Street,
London WC2E 7BN.
Tel: 071 240 0953.

(*Self-help support groups for lone parents*)

Home-Start Consultancy,
2 Salisbury Road,
Leicester LE1 7QR.
Tel: 0533 554988.

(*Practical help/befriending for parents with a child under 5*)

International Planned Parenthood Federation,
18-20 Lower Regent Street,
London SW1.

(*Full family planning information across countries and religions*)

Married Gays
c/o London Friend,
274 Upper Street,
London N1.
Tel: 071 837 7324.

(*Support line*)

MIND,
22 Harley Street,
London W1N 2ED.
Tel: 071 637 0741.

(*Information and advice for people with mental health difficulties and their families*)

Narcotics Anonymous,
PO Box 417,
London SW10 0RS.
Tel: 071 351 6794.

(*Self-help groups for people with a drug problem*)

National Association for Maternal and Child Welfare,
18 South Audley Street,
London W1Y 6JS.
Tel: 071 491 2772.

(*Help and advice for families and children*)

National Childbirth Trust,
Alexandra House,
Oldham Terrace,
London W3 6NH.
Tel: 081 992 8637.

(*Information support in pregnancy, childbirth and early parenthood. Also aims to enable parents to make informed choices*)

National Children's Bureau,
8 Wakeley Street,
London EC1V 7QE.
Tel: 071 278 9441.

(*Wide-ranging, constantly updated information service on all aspects of childhood disability*)

National Council for One Parent Families,
255 Kentish Town Road,
Camden,
London NW5 2LX.
Tel: 071 267 1361.

(*Help, support, information*)

National Marriage Council,
PO Box 4000,
Glasgow G12.
Tel: 041 248 5249.

(*Information, help and advice on marriage counselling given to single and married people and all couples*)

National Schizophrenia Fellowship,
28 Castle Street,
Kingston-upon-Thames,
Surrey KT1 1SS.
Tel: 081 547 3937.

(*Support groups for sufferers and their families*)

National Stepfamily Association,
72 Willesden Lane,
London NW6 7TA.
Tel: 081 372 0844.

(*Help, advice, information*)

NEWPIN (New Parent Infant Network),
Sutherland House,
Sutherland Square,
Southwark,
London SE17 3EE.
Tel: 071 703 5271.

(*Help, advice, information*)

NSPCC (National Society for the Prevention of Cruelty to Children),
Tel: 0792 41795.

(*Help, guidance and support for parents in difficulty*)

Parent Network,
44–46 Cavisham Road,
London NW5 2AD.
Tel: 071 485 8535.

(*Support group for parents wanting to get on better with their children and with each other*)

Parents' Anonymous,
Parentline,
Rayfa House,
57 Hart Road,
Thundersley,
Essex SS7 3PD.
Tel: 0268 757077.

(*Telephone support for parents under stress*)

Rape Crisis,
London Tel: 071 837 1600. (Will refer to local centres).

(*Support, advice, telephone counselling for women and girls who have been raped or sexually assaulted [and for their families]*)

Relate Marriage Guidance,
Hubert Gray College,
Little Church Street,
Rugby,
Warwickshire CV21 3AP.
Tel: 0788 73241.

(*Appointments and counselling for married and single people*)

Salvation Army Tracing Missing Relatives Branch,
110/112 Middlesex Street,
London E1 7HZ.
Tel: 071 247 6831.

Samaritans (in local telephone directories)
London Tel: 071 439 2224.

(*Telephone help-line for people in crisis or longer-term emotional pain*)

Survivors
Tel: 071 833 3737 (part time – keep trying)

(*Support, advice, counselling for men and boys who have been raped or sexually assaulted*)

Terence Higgins Trust,
52-54 Grays Inn Road,
London WC1X 8JU.
Tel: 071 242 1010.

(*Information, advice, help on AIDS and HIV infection. Also family support*)

Women's Aid Federation (England),
374 Grays Inn Road,
Camden,
London WC1 8BB.
Tel: 071 837 9316.

(*Legal help and advice. Referrals for women with or without children to refuges*)

USA, Canada, Australia and other countries

As the distances, areas and conurbations are so diverse and the resources often locally named, it is not possible to give a useful, up-to-date list of particular numbers. Obviously small countries may be sadly deficient in adequate help centres. However the organizations below are certainly international and if your library or local radio station cannot help, here might be a place to start – depending on your problem. Check your directory for local telephone numbers.

Al-Anon Family Groups
For families of people with a drink problem

Alcoholics Anonymous

For people with a drink problem

Families Anonymous
also *Naranon*

(For families of people with a suspected, current or former drug problem)

Narcotics Anonymous

For people with a drug problem

Parents Anonymous/Parentline

(For parents under stress)

Samaritans – Befrienders International

(Telephone support for people in crisis or with long term emotional difficulties)

Further reading

Ariès, Philippe: *Centuries of Childhood*, Penguin 1973

Bettelheim, Bruno: *A Good Enough Parent*, Thames & Hudson 1987

Bethune, Helen: *Off the Hook: Coping with Addiction*, Methuen 1985

Bowlby, John: *Childcare and the Growth of Love*, Pelican 1953

Consumers' Association: *Children, Parents and the Law*, Which? Nov. 1985

Freud, Sigmund: Various books and papers

Illich, Ivan: *Deschooling Society*, Penguin 1970

Joshi, Heather: *The Cash Opportunity Costs of Childbearing: an approach using British data*, Discussion series paper no 208; Centre for Economic Policy Research

Huizinga, Johan: *Homo Ludens – A Study of the Play Element in Culture*, Routledge & Kegan Paul 1949

Jung, Carl Gustav: *Collected Works*, Routledge & Kegan Paul 1978

Masson, Jeffrey: *Freud: The Assault on Truth*, Faber 1984

Miller, Alice: *Thou Shalt Not Be Aware*, Pluto 1985

Peck, M. Scott: *The Road Less Travelled*, Hutchinson 1983

Pinchbeck, D & Hewitt, M.: *Children in English Society*, Routledge & Kegan Paul 1973

Powell, John: *Why Am I Afraid to Tell You Who I Am?*, Argus 1969

Registrar General's *Annual Statistics Review*, HMSO

Spock, Dr Benjamin: *Baby & Child Care*, Bodley Head 1960

Taub-Bynum, E. Bruce: *The Family Unconscious*, Quest 1984

Thornton, E.M.: *Freud and Cocaine*, Blond & Briggs 1983

Whitfield, Charles L.: *Healing the Child Within*, Health Communications 1987

Winnicott, D.W.: *The Child, the Family and the Outside World*, Pelican 1984

Index